EMBRACING
GRACE

Marlys Johnson poignantly recounts (with wit and humor) her own remarkable journey from an early more untested life of dramatic answers to prayer and faith-building experiences to a much more challenging life fraught with difficulties and heartbreak. Through it all her honesty and faith offers hope to us all.

Dr. Andre J. Snodgrass

EMBRACING
GRACE

Experiencing Joy in the Journey of Life

MARLYS JOHNSON

A DIVISION OF DEEP RIVER BOOKS

Trusted Books is an imprint of Deep River Books. The views expressed or implied in this work are those of the author. To learn more about Deep River Books, go online to www.DeepRiverBooks.com.

Unless otherwise noted, all Scriptures are taken from the *Holy Bible, New International Version˙ Study Bible, NIV*. Copyright © 2002 Zondervan. All rights reserved. Book introductions used with permission. General Editor: Kenneth L. Barker.

ISBN 13: 978-1-63269-015-9
Library of Congress Catalog Card Number: 2012916459

This book is dedicated to my husband,
Dave Johnson.
You are not only the love of my life,
but you believed in me even when I didn't believe in myself.

CONTENTS

Introduction. ix

1. Open Hands 1
2. Small Beginnings 13
3. Artichoke 23
4. Incomprehensible. 35
5. Ducks. 41
6. Ask. 49
7. Beyond Expectations 57
8. The List 65
9. Shadows. 71
10. Valley 79
11. Tough Love vs. Grace 95
12. Struggles. 101
13. Sunshine 105

14. Hope 109

15. Restoration. 115

16. Grief. 123

17. Loving Kindness and Mercy. 131

18. Heaven's Door 139

19. Promise 147

INTRODUCTION

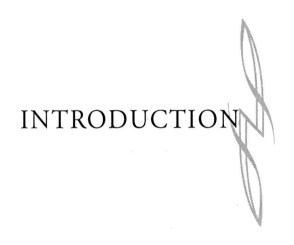

A S A PRIVATE high school math teacher, I was allowed to slip in Bible verses or short faith stories from my life as time allowed. Students grabbed onto these stories and verses and began applying them to their lives.

One student commented, "Remember that story you shared about praying over physics tests? Well, after you told your story, I decided to let God help me with a very difficult test. I was over-the-top nervous about the test. And God really did help me. He did! He calmed me down and helped me think logically. I was so excited. Mrs. Johnson, you need to get these stories written down in a book."

Two years ago when I checked Zoey into the dog kennels maintained by our Purdy women's prison system, a visitor won my heart by exclaiming over Zoey's cuteness. We dog owners take such praises quite personally. When I shared how the dog originally belonged to Bryna, our daughter who had passed away only a year before, the conversation turned to eating disorders, the grieving process, and the love of Jesus. "You need to write a book. Now! Parents need encouragement. Teens need truths." Her words echoed in my mind for months after that conversation.

I do not feel like a gifted writer. Good grief! I accidentally majored in physics while earning my bachelor's degree, and I teach calculus. I play with numbers, not words! However, my heart is heavy for the pain I see in people wrestling through eating disorders, drug addictions, abuse, marriage issues, faith questions, and grief over huge losses. Authors today have been a huge source of encouragement in my own faith journey; I hope to speak words of encouragement into the hearts of others.

My faith, built on a shaky foundation, was torn to shreds. As I struggled with God over seeming contradictions in the Bible, He brought truth into my life. Having a relationship with God and experiencing some amazing answers to prayer did not spare me from walking through dark, dark times. If God had not been with me during those hard times, I shudder to think of where my journey would have taken me. He has made all the difference!

God's handprints are all over my life; His hugs are everywhere I turn. I pray that this book can be an extension of God's hug to you.

Chapter 1

OPEN HANDS

HEADING THROUGH THE living room on my way into the kitchen, I glanced over my shoulder at our infant daughter, who was supposedly asleep in her crib. Instead, I saw Stacey lying flat on her back, thrashing her head violently from side to side, with no sound coming out of her mouth. Her skin was a reddish-purplish color as she fought to breathe. Reacting with predictable parental panic, I grabbed her up and threw her over my shoulder, pounding on her back. Still no sound came from her mouth. I pounded; she was silent. Suddenly, she let out her own cries of panic. There we were; Stacey, crying out of her trauma, and me, praising God and saying, "Thank you, thank you, thank you, God." My heart was full of gratefulness as she cried and I rejoiced.

At the hospital when she was born, I was in the maternity ward while the pediatrician was making his routine checks on the newborns. "Everything is great except for one thing."

Time stood still. My mind raced ahead, imagining that the "one thing" might be a missing finger or extra toe, or even worse, a damaged heart or leukemia or some horrible disease. The mind can come up with so many things within a split second of time.

The doctor continued, "She has a cleft palate." Suddenly the cleft palate sounded so minor compared to the myriad of things it could have been. Little did I know how debilitating and life threatening a cleft palate could be if it impaired an infant's ability to eat or breathe.

Reading through cleft palate literature, I learned clefts can start at the palate and go no further, or continue on through the gum and stop there, or continue on through the lips. Likewise, the reverse order can occur. Fortunately, Stacey had only a cleft palate with no facial disfigurement. She was a beautiful baby girl. I responded to the doctor's "Only one thing wrong" diagnosis with "No big deal." I was so wrong!

Nurses instructed me how to use a breast shield and baby bottle nipples for premature infants so I could feed her my breast milk. She was a full-term baby, but the cleft in her palate reduced her ability to suck. By the third day in the hospital, my milk had come in and the staff assured me Stacey had taken in two ounces of milk. It looked like everything was going great. However, after the next feeding they told me she had not taken in any milk. The feedings were basically identical; they must have made an error in their measurements. Stacey looked calm and peaceful, and I felt assured she was getting the nutrition she needed. Apparently the hospital staff felt she needed a longer time to nurse. So, with this encouragement, they sent me home. A home nurse was assigned to me who would be making routine visits to check on Stacey's progress.

On that fateful afternoon when Stacey almost died, I continued praising God while comforting her. My mind raced forward to the coming night. What if Stacey should stop breathing during the night? If she were in the dining room, I would never hear her. Obviously, I needed to place her beside my bed so I could help her if she had breathing issues.

Stacey had one of the widest clefts that therapists had seen in Tacoma's speech and therapy specialized care of Mary Bridge Children's Hospital. Because breathing while lying on a flat, horizontal surface was difficult for Stacey, we had her bed inclined and even changed her diapers on the incline. As she gradually slid down the incline, we picked up speed in the diaper change. It was quite a feat to change diapers on a moving target. Out of curiosity, we timed how long she could be comfortable lying flat on her back. The longest she could lie on the horizontal before choking and sputtering was fifty-five seconds.

Feeding her was definitely a challenge. When I first brought her home, I thought she could drink through the apparatus the hospital developed for us. I thought they made a mistake when they told me Stacey did not get any milk on my last feeding. Unfortunately, the mistake was recording two ounces in the previous feeding. She was not getting food from my breasts. I stayed up all night nursing her. By five a.m. I was exhausted, the household was waking up for a new day, and I was still nursing her. Stacey's skin had turned a bluish color and felt cold. My mom swaddled her in more blankets while I contacted the assigned nurse. She told me to go to an animal feed store and buy a lamb's nipple.

Feeling quite out of place in an animal feed store, I asked,

"I came to buy a lamb's nipple. Can you show me where you have them?"

"So do you have sheep?"

"No, I have a baby person."

We tried the lamb's nipple with partial success. Stacey was still not getting milk. She seemed to be dying in front of us. I called the surgeon who would be working with us in about a year. I anxiously asked,

"Is there anything we can do? We can't wait a year. I feel like my baby is dying!"

He calmly replied,

"There is only one way to feed your baby. You need to get a plastic baby bottle and, using a sterilized, hot needle, burn a bigger hole in the nipple. Hand express your milk into the bottle and then gently squeeze the plastic bottle so the stream of milk will go into her mouth."

Brilliant! So simple, but brilliant! It worked. Stacey was one very hungry infant. How rewarding to see her fill up on milk and then fall asleep.

However, we had to be very careful in gently squeezing the bottle. With the cleft palate, she coughed and sputtered as milk poured out her nose. Feedings were long and required a great amount of patience. In fact, the four p.m. feeding went pretty much nonstop until one a.m. if it were a quick feeding and three a.m. if it were a slow feeding. We continually had to suction out her nose to clear out passageways and help her through the coughing and sputtering.

To further complicate matters, Lynell was one and a half years old and full of energy. Life was wonderful and there were a thousand things she wanted to do all at once. Characteristically, she sprang into action about 5:30 a.m. Do the math! Stacey finally falls asleep between one and three a.m. and Lynell gets up at 5:30 a.m. So, when does Mom get her sleep? My husband was working full time and going to school, and the dog and cat were of little help.

As I processed these many issues on that fateful afternoon in the dining room while I was calming Stacey down, the question, again, was "What if Stacey quits breathing during the night?"

I decided I needed to move her right next to my bed where I could tend to her when needed. The solution did not work so well. Cleft palate children are very noisy as they try to sleep. Every time I drifted off to sleep, she made a snorting noise, and I jerked into alarm mode from my almost-asleep mode, thinking she was unable to breathe. But she was fine. As I continued to doze off, another snort or cough or sputter had me diving over her bed to see if something was wrong. I spent my whole short night jumping out of every attempt to sleep. Morning came and I was exhausted; totally spent; at the end of myself.

I couldn't play with Lynell, wash diapers, fold laundry, prepare meals, and care for Stacey all during the day and then perform guard duty all night. We did not have fetal monitors in those days. I did not know what to do. Desperate, broken, alone, I flopped down on my bed and sobbed. But I didn't cry solely to myself. I had learned through the years that crying to myself gets really messy, stuffs up my head, and makes my eyes puffy. It may release some tension, but doesn't really solve things. Instead, I cried to myself a bit and then I cried to God. I told Him I couldn't do it. I couldn't be the mom I needed to be. There was no way I could watch over Stacey during the night and still be the mom to my kids and a wife of my husband in the waking hours. I was running on empty. I was at the end of myself.

"I know these children do not belong to me," I told God. "They belong to You. They are blessings You have given us to parent. I want to close my fist around these children, hold them close, and not let anything take them away from me, but I know I need to open my hand and trust them to Your purposes. You have loaned them to us to raise. They do not belong to us. They belong to You. Oh God, I can't keep Stacey alive."

While I was pouring out my thoughts to God, Brother Andrew's experience with smuggling Bibles flashed in my mind. He had his Volkswagen loaded with Bibles to transport across the Rumanian border. With only a half-dozen cars in front of him, he did not expect a long wait. But after the first car took nearly an hour to investigate, he wondered if each car would be submitted to such a thorough investigation. He watched as drivers were told to stand outside their car as hubcaps and seats were removed and the car scrutinized. Literally everything the families were carrying had to be taken out and spread on the ground. Knowing it would only take seconds for guards to discover his trunk stuffed with Bibles, he recognized the hopelessness of his situation. With only one car in front of him, he prayed, "Dear Jesus, just as You made blind eyes see, I pray today that You will make seeing eyes blind." To let Jesus know that his trust was completely in Jesus rescuing him, and not with any cleverness on his part, he took six Bibles out of hiding and placed them in a stack next to his seat. After watching the intense searches for four hours, he then inched forward for his turn at being inspected. Handing papers to the guard, he started to get out of the car. But the guard's knee pressed against his car door, holding it closed. The guard examined his passport, scribbled something down, and shoved the papers back to Brother Andrew. He then motioned for him to drive forward. As he moved forward, he glanced in his rearview mirror at the motorist behind him, getting out of his car for the guards to inspect. He continued to move forward, wondering exactly where he was supposed to park his car. No one seemed to notice him. He continued moving forward and discovered to his amazement that he had crossed the border in thirty seconds with all his Bibles snugly intact.

"Dear God, I lift Stacey up to You. I want to stand guard over her every second of every day, but I can't do that. Only You can do that. What are Your purposes for her life? Have You loaned her to us for only a brief moment? We don't own her, for she belongs to You. But we thank You for allowing us to be her parents. We treasure this life You have called us to parent. If You intend to take Stacey, I open my hands, and You can take her. She belongs to You and it will be well with my soul. But God, I need You to know that it is my desire that You let us raise this beloved child. At this point, if You want us to raise this child, then I trust You will bring me to her side when she needs me, just like You brought me to her side yesterday when I wasn't even intending to check on her. And as a step of my faith and trust in You, I am going to move her back into the dining room where I can't possibly hear her at night. If she needs my presence during the night, I trust You will let me know just like You did yesterday."

The above prayer might seem like child neglect or foolishness to someone who has not known the enormous fatigue of pouring out one's life for babies. I couldn't do more than I was doing. I was alone in the daily care of my children. I was helpless. I felt like the mother sheep in Isaiah 40:11 baaing to my Good Shepherd, Jesus Christ, who looked for the little lambs tangled in briars. He picked up those little ones and held them close to His chest, while the mother sheep looked on with gratefulness. Since mother sheep do not have the proper anatomy for picking up their young and untangling them from the briars, they were helpless in their ability to assist their lambs. I felt like a mother sheep baaing for the Good Shepherd to come to the rescue of my lamb, for whom I could not adequately care. This Isaiah 40:11 prayer would repeat itself throughout my life.

Why didn't I call my friends and organize a team of nighttime guards to watch over Stacey? I don't know. Maybe the Holy Spirit was nudging me to leave Stacey in Jesus' hands. I don't know the answers to all these questions. All I know is that prayer changed me.

I was totally unprepared for the result of my prayer. When I poured out this prayer to Jesus, a deep, deep peace came over me and sank into the marrow of my bones. All my anxieties and fatigue instantly left me. I felt a peace that surpasses all understanding and is beyond human words to describe. It took me totally by surprise. I had never experienced this before and would come to experience it many more times in my parenting. But this was the first time. It was indescribable. I did not know if Stacey would live or if God would take her. The peace I experienced was deeper than sedatives before surgery. It was unshakeable and went down into the core of my being. I knew without a shadow of doubt that God's perfect will would be accomplished. I knew God would be with us no matter what. It was truly well with my soul!

Today, I am happy to report, Stacey is a mother of four children. She survived her infancy! I also need to add, lest one might conclude that all prayers are answered the way we want them to be answered, that God would one day ask me to open my hand and let one of my children go to Him. But at this time, Stacey was here to stay.

I slept my short nights in a deep sleep and God gave me a strength and immunity that were not my own. I need eight or nine hours of sleep to be sane. If I get short on sleep, colds and viruses grab me and take me captive. For the first three years of Stacey's life, God gave me a miraculous protection against all sicknesses. My family members came down with all kinds of colds and viruses, while I remained healthy. Eventually, when Stacey was five years old, I got one of those ten-day colds. But until then, I might have a ten-hour cold, but nothing worse. I had been one of those strange high school kids who always contracted a cold after two days of great fun on a youth group outing. So, when I report my health in those trying days with so little sleep, I am reporting a miracle.

When Stacey was fifteen months old, she was scheduled for her first of seven cleft palate surgeries. To fix the cleft in one big surgery would result in a high risk of facial deformity where her face would gradually take on the characteristics of a "dish plate" face. I am not sure what that would look like, but I didn't want it for Stacey.

Dave and I were relatively calm during the first hour and a half of her surgery. The doctor had explained that the procedure would take about one and a half hours. As the time stretched into two hours and then two and a half hours, our calmness gradually dissipated. Even the speech therapist who had worked with Stacey since her birth and who was waiting with us grew noticeably nervous. Finally the doctor called and informed us that once he was into the surgery, he realized the cleft was so huge that doing a series of surgeries would give her permanent speech impairment. So, risking facial deformity, he closed the cleft in one big surgery. Stacey is now a grown adult and her face is beautiful—no dish plate!! And her speech therapy, which was supposed to continue until kindergarten, was discontinued much earlier. Oh my goodness! Two weeks after her surgery, when her mouth had healed so that she wanted to talk, she spoke in complete sentences. I had no idea she knew any words other than "mama" and "dada." And here she was talking in complete sentences. Obviously, she had been talking in complete sentences before the surgery, but all her words were unrecognizable due to the cleft in her palate. My heart goes out to those children with clefts in their palates who live in cultures where surgery is not a possibility. They struggle to communicate, but no one can understand them.

By the time she was four, I told God that He overdid the prayer answers for clear speech. The child would not stop talking. She continued in monologues, never ending sentences with a period, but with the magic word "and" so that she could continue talking with run-on sentences forever, not to be interrupted by siblings vying for their turn to talk.

Other issues for children with cleft palates include constant earaches and ruptures. We went through the ruptures and ear tubes and waiting rooms. One particular visit to a specialist stands out in my memory. After looking inside both her ears, the doctor asked me if Stacey could hear out of her left ear. I had no idea! Who checks that? I had never thought to check. He ordered hearing tests and we waited for the results. When called into his office, Stacey and I perched in front of his mahogany desk, waiting silently as he shuffled through papers. He looked up from the folder and exclaimed, "It's a miracle." Then he looked down again at his charts. We said nothing. Looking up at us again, he repeated, "It's a miracle." And he returned to his papers.

Finally, he looked at me and said, "It's a miracle. I saw so much scarring from ruptures in her left ear that I thought she could not hear at all from her left ear. But this report says she has perfect hearing in her left ear." Yowee! We sang praises to God for the entire one-hour trip back home.

What am I saying? Prayers do make a difference. God hears our prayers and answers. They don't always get answered the way we want them to, but God is always with us. He does not desert us. If we seek Him, we will find Him. And He makes all the difference. I don't want anyone reading this to assume that I am saying that prayer and faith result in a life of roses and sunshine. Not every cleft palate child survives. Not every baby lives. God's ways are not our ways. But He is our loving Heavenly Father and He makes a huge difference in our lives, whatever the circumstances, if we let Him walk with us.

Chapter 2

SMALL BEGINNINGS

SO WHERE DOES faith come from? My dad, who claimed to be an atheist when he married my mom, taught me the bedtime prayer:

Now I lay me down to sleep;
I pray my Lord my soul to keep.
If I should die before I wake,
I pray, oh Lord, my soul to take.

As a preschool child, I think the only part of this prayer I understood was that I was going to sleep and God was somewhere out there in space. I had no idea what a soul was, and dying had not entered my brain.

When students in my first-grade class talked about Sunday school, I asked my parents if I could go to Sunday school like my friends did. My dad figured that Sunday school would not hurt me, selected the closest church to our house, and sent me on the six-block walk to church. Teachers unrolled a huge paper scroll with the week's selected memory verse while we earned prizes for reciting it.

As a third grader, I joined my younger siblings, Lois and Bruce, journeying a couple miles to another church, which better met our parents' approval. Even though religion was not discussed at home, we listened to our teachers and believed all they told us. We frequently had squabbles with each other on the way to church. Not having any adult around to voice one's complaints, the angry person resorted to walking a half block behind the other two of us. However, after hearing the lesson for the day, we were always much better friends on the way back home.

One yard sign troubled us. It read, "Keep off the grass. Trespassers will be prosecuted." I thought "prosecuted" was "persecuted." And when Christ was persecuted, He was crucified on the cross. So, I logically explained to my siblings that we had to stay off the grass or we would be hung on a cross. That seemed like such a stiff penalty for walking on the grass. But we did show great respect for the grass.

Scripture verses taught from the King James version were also a bit confusing. In Matthew 6: 5,6 it says,

"And when thou prayest, thou shalt not be as the hypocrites are:
for they love to pray standing in the synagogues
and in the corners of the streets, that they may be seen of men.
Verily I say unto you, They have their reward.
But thou, when thou prayest, enter into thy closet,
and when thou hast shut thy door,
pray to thy Father which is in secret;
And thy Father which seeth in secret
Shall reward thee openly."

Now that was a tough verse to carry out. Lois and I shared a basement bedroom with a closet built under the stairs. The sloping ceiling allowed barely enough room to sit. With no light in the closet, I crawled through the dirt and perched on a luggage bag to pray. If I sat up straight, my head would touch the sloping ceiling. As you might imagine, my prayer was short. The closet was dark and stuffy. When I found my way back out of the closet, I dusted off the cobwebs and wondered what was so special about a closet.

And then there was the passage about giving water to Jesus. In Matthew 25:31–46, it says,

> When the Son of Man comes in his glory, and all the angels with him, he will sit on his throne in heavenly glory. All the nations will be gathered before him, and he will separate the people one from another as a shepherd separates the sheep from the goats. He will put the sheep on his right and the goats on his left.
>
> Then the King will say to those on his right, "Come, you who are blessed by my Father; take your inheritance, the kingdom prepared for you since the creation of the world. For I was hungry and you gave me something to eat, I was thirsty and you gave me something to drink, I was a stranger and you invited me in, I needed clothes and you clothed me, I was sick and you looked after me, I was in prison and you came to visit me."
>
> Then the righteous will answer him, "Lord, when did we see you hungry and feed you, or thirsty and give you something to drink? When did we see you a stranger and invite you in, or needing clothes and clothe you? When did we see you sick or in prison and go to visit you?"

The King will reply, "I tell you the truth, whatever you did for one of the least of these brothers of mine, you did for me."

Then he will say to those on his left, "Depart from me, you who are cursed, into the eternal fire prepared for the devil and his angels. For I was hungry and you gave me nothing to eat, I was thirsty and you gave me nothing to drink, I was a stranger and you did not invite me in, I needed clothes and you did not clothe me, I was sick and in prison and you did not look after me."

Giving clothes away and visiting prisoners and ministering to the sick went right over the top of my head. The concept of how we treat people is how we treat Jesus also whisked right past my brain cells. But I was ready to help Jesus if He was thirsty. So, Lois and Bruce and I decided to give Jesus water. We had three aluminum glasses stored in a low bathroom cupboard. We carefully filled up the glasses with water, placed them back in the cupboard, and left the room so Jesus could have a drink. We kept checking the water level, and it did not seem to move. Deciding that Jesus was not yet thirsty, we left the glasses for a couple days. He still did not drink. I must say that the process of evaporation is immeasurably slow! So we dumped out the water and remained mystified as to how to give Jesus water.

Although God did not drink from our water glasses, He did reveal Himself to me. I am not at all proud of my first interaction with God, but it has made a huge imprint on my life. When I was six years old, God interrupted my sleep in the early morning hours by opening my mouth wide and locking my jaw so that I could not close my mouth. He had my attention as I imagined trying to explain to my mom, without using any words, that I could not close my mouth.

He then said something like, "Don't tell lies." I don't remember His exact wording and I don't think He used a lot of sentences. I don't know what His voice sounded like, but it was audible to my ears, not something I heard in my head. I knew it was God speaking. And then He unlocked my jaw. I was frightened and relieved. The next day I found myself stopping midsentence so many times. I was in such a habit of lying that I lied about all kinds of things. I was not lying just to get out of trouble. I was lying as a lifestyle. I might say I have six dollars when I have only four dollars or the sidewalk was gray when it was really some other color. My conversation was full of exaggerations and lies. I began working hard to speak words of truth. Even as an adult, I have struggled to speak the truth. Sometimes I imagine doing something wrong and intentionally practice saying, "Yes, I did that."

As a high school teacher, I often told inspirational stories to my classroom. I was so afraid of embellishing the truth that I ordered radio cassettes of the stories I wanted to share. I transcribed the story, sentence by sentence, so I had a hard copy from which I could memorize the story and then retell my students. I feel like I have a weakness for lying, and I want to follow God's commandment to me for telling the truth.

Another interaction with God involved a red coin purse. It was a red plastic coin purse attached to a small gold chain. There was a red flap that snapped over the coin purse. Dollar bills could be stored in that flap, but, more importantly, there was a small clear plastic window showing the identification card where I had neatly printed my name, address, and phone number. I loved twirling my red coin purse round and round my finger as I jaunted to the neighborhood store.

That coin purse went just about everywhere with me. It made its way to a camping trip on the ocean. And for some odd reason, it accompanied me as I jumped from log to log on the beach. And then, somewhere in the log jumping, it departed. I did not miss it until we were packing up to leave for home. My purse was gone!

I hurried back to the beach and searched everywhere. My family eventually joined me, everyone looking for my little red purse. Unfortunately, dusk crept in and it became more difficult to tell whether we were looking at dark shadows or tree limbs. My dad called an end to the search. I was devastated. It never occurred to me that we might not find it. I knew we would. And now we were leaving without the purse. I ran back to our tent and fell on my knees in prayer. "Lord, please help me find my coin purse."

Through the years, my dad has retold the rest of my story with more details than I remembered. He watched me walk out of the tent and down to the beach. He watched as I walked directly to a huge log that was about two and a half feet in diameter. With some effort, I climbed on top of it and then walked a few steps down the log. I knelt down, laid down crosswise over the log, scooted on my stomach so I could reach down under the log where I could not even see anything, and pulled up the purse. I had gone straight from the tent to the purse. No way? OK, God's way!

Another time, when I was about eight years old, a sick goldfish wiggled its way into my life. While my parents were visiting my grandparents, I sat and stared at a poor little sick goldfish in the glass bowl. He would float upside down, looking totally dead, and then flick his tail and try a shallow fish dive, only to end up floating upside down again. I watched him for the longest time and was so sad over his feeble attempts at swimming. My grandfather had spotted this sick fish in his outdoor goldfish pond and transferred him into the indoor goldfish bowl. When he was sure the fish had died, he carted the bowl out to the backyard, where he dug a hole to bury the fish. But when he placed the fish in the dirt hole, the fish flicked his tail! So Grandpa picked up the fish and returned it to the bowl. The trauma of waking up in a dirt hole should have killed the fish! So by the time I saw the fish, he had been sick a number of days. Returning home, I was consumed with sadness for this struggling fish. I retreated downstairs to my bedroom and prayed God would heal the fish. Finding my mom in the kitchen fixing dinner, I told her that I had prayed for the fish and God was going to heal the fish. Minutes later, really and truly, only minutes later, my grandmother called and she was so excited. "I don't know what happened, but the fish is swimming all over the bowl. He looks totally fine." Ever so often afterward, my grandmother would take me to her pond and point out the fish I had prayed for. That fish grew to be about one and a half times longer than any other fish in the pond. It was like the fish was screaming at me, "God is real and God answers prayers."

A myriad of other prayers were answered in my growing-up years. But these three—God speaking, the coin purse, and the goldfish—were the anchors God gave me in my life.

So what is this all about? Why does God heal a goldfish? Why does He bother with a coin purse? I thought He had more important things to do. What about the starving children in Uganda, the homeless in my city, the person down the street with cancer? How does finding a coin purse compare to these gut-wrenching needs? Isn't God too busy with important things to be bothered with coin purses and goldfish? Apparently He isn't! Apparently He is bigger than I can perceive. Psalm 139:1–4 says, "O LORD, you have searched me and you know me. You know when I sit and when I rise; you perceive my thoughts from afar. You discern my going out and my lying down; you are familiar with all my ways. Before a word is on my tongue you know it completely, O LORD."

He knows us, because He has created us. He knows us better than we know ourselves. He loves us more than we can comprehend. We put Him in a box and think He can only answer "x" number of prayers at one time. Whatever number we put in for "x," He is bigger than we think. He answers goldfish prayers and lost purse prayers as well as the big prayers.

At this time, some of you are thinking about the big prayers He did not answer. Things did not go as you desperately hoped. Hey, I have a couple of those prayers also. And I will address them further in this book. But for right now, let us rejoice in our Heavenly Father who loves us a thousand times more than we love ourselves and delights in us. One of my favorite verses is Psalm 139:17, "How precious to me are your thoughts, O God! How vast is the sum of them! Were I to count them, they would outnumber the grains of sand."

How much do we believe that verse? Would you replace "grains of sand" with much smaller numbers represented by "eggs in an egg carton" or "traffic lights between home and work" or "toothbrushes we buy in a lifetime" or "meals we have cooked?" How big is God?

I love to go on four-mile prayer runs from my house. We live on a huge "block" in Gig Harbor. Running around the block is a four-mile trek. Once I get past the halfway mark, there is no turning back. When I am running alone, there are no phones to interrupt me, no surprise knocks on the door, no distracting music. I run and converse with God. I do better listening to God when I am all out of breath! Sometimes I leave for these runs with my heart weighed down from impossible situations. I see no solutions and feel deeply perplexed about my next course of action. I take off running, articulating to God my feelings and troubles. And then I listen. I ask questions. I argue. I listen. And the amazing result is that I often return with new hope, new direction, and a specific action I need to do. I have had an individual counseling session with Jesus. One time, after such an experience, I was sharing with my friend about the special fellowship time I had enjoyed with God during my run that day. She immediately responded with a similar story she experienced at the same time. My finite mind asks, "How can that be? How can she be having a special one-on-one time with God at the same time I am having a special one-on-one time with God? And for that matter, how can thousands of people around the world feel like they are having special one-on-one times with God all at the same time?" Oh my goodness, are your brain neurons jumping like crazy?

God cares about the details of our lives. We see the grace of God when we experience answers to the purse and goldfish prayers of our lives.

Chapter 3

ARTICHOKE

THROUGH MY GROWING-UP years, my faith grew from answered prayers, Bible stories, and Bible teachers. I believed everything my Bible teachers told me. I loved reading the stories about the Good Shepherd finding the lost sheep, and the paralyzed man walking again. Great people poured their lives into my life, leading me down the path of faith. One of those influential people was my dad.

Daddy announced one day, "These kids are growing up so fast and I am not spending time with them." As an ambitious realtor, he did not have chunks of time to spend with us. To remedy the situation, he decided to go on walks with us before school. Three blocks away, the railroad tracks led us on a two-mile trek to my grandparents' house. My dad was an unusual one. He decided running along the tops of the boxcars of a stationary train and then jumping from car to car was much more fun that running down the tracks. So, he had all of us climbing up on top of those boxcars, running down the metal gratings, and then jumping from car to car like crazy people. We left early in the morning so we could get to my grandparents' house, say "hello" for no more than ten minutes, and return home in time for a big breakfast and short walk to school. Since we began our walk while most responsible people were still sleeping, all the dogs from various yards would join us, venture to our grandparents', and then return to their own homes one by one on our return trip. Occasionally we ended up with an extra dog that forgot to leave our group, and then my mom begrudgingly packed up the dog and returned it to its home.

Other mornings, we left at four a.m. with all our fishing poles, and walked over a mile to Wapato Lake, where we caught our fish for breakfast. During these trips, my dad, who was no longer an atheist, would join hands with us at Wapato Lake and lead us in prayer, with each one of us praying out loud. We never did this in any other place outside of Wapato Park. I was in the fourth grade when he introduced this idea to us, and I began memorizing passages from Psalms in the Bible so I would know how to pray. Although he did not verbalize his faith to us, he lived it. Years later we heard from various people how my dad ministered to them.

In high school, Bruce took on a job of bussing tables at Point Defiance Grill. Noticing Bruce's name tag, one customer asked him if he knew Roy Farrington.

"He is my dad."

"Roy Farrington is the best friend I ever had. What is your name?"

"Bruce."

"You don't know who I am, do you?"

"No, I don't."

"I was on the streets, begging money from your dad so that I could indulge in alcohol. I wanted to go drinking. But instead of giving me money, your dad took me to a Chinese restaurant for lunch. This seemed like risky business to me, because a businessman does not want to be seen lunching with a drunk. He talked with me about where I was going in my life and what I needed to do. He did this lunch talk with me, not once, but many, many times. I have been clean for ten years. He saved my life and he was the best friend I ever had."

We never knew anything about such stories in my dad's life, for he never talked about what he was doing. When I worked at the real estate office for a couple weeks each summer, I heard various stories from customers. One person told me how he met with an elderly lady who wanted to list her home for sale. Her kitchen sink was piled high with dirty dishes and things were in total disarray. My dad, who never cleaned up our kitchen to my remembrance, jumped in, washed her dishes, and helped her restore order.

Even though Daddy did not verbally expound on his faith, he instilled in me a respect and trust toward the adults in my life. It was therefore easy for me to believe and trust my Sunday school teachers. There would come the day when my belief system would be shattered.

My mom also helped me along this faith journey. Even though my family experienced many answers to prayer, I was troubled by the "no answered" ones. My mom helped me work through this. One day, Lois, Bruce, and I decided to give our miniature pet turtle a day outside in the sunshine. Since a small green turtle in green grass can easily be overlooked, we picked off dandelion flower heads and placed them carefully behind him to mark his slow progress. A yellow dandelion trail curved through our front yard. Apparently losing his enchantment of the hike in the grass, he stopped, and thus halted our dandelion game. Boring! So we entertained ourselves with somersaulting down the hill in our front yard. We checked up on slow turtle a number of times, and no progress was made. And then, something happened. When we checked on him again, he was totally missing. No turtle in sight. We looked everywhere. How could we have lost him? We prayed, and we were deeply troubled. No turtle. How can that be? If we prayed, why didn't the turtle return? My mom took that opportunity to explain away my Santa Claus concept of God by telling me sometimes God says, "Yes," sometimes He says, "Wait," and sometimes, He says, "No, I have a better plan." The interesting part of this story is that about three or four years later, a family three houses away discovered a rather large turtle in their outdoor fishpond. They had no idea of how a turtle ended up in their pond. In Texas, turtles were out in the wild. But in the Pacific Northwest, we don't have outdoor turtles roaming about. So, how did a turtle appear in the fishpond three houses away and where did our turtle go? Did our tiny little turtle make a three-house journey on those little legs? I don't know. That is one question I hope to ask in heaven. There are some more!

My parents lived honorably, and by their example, taught me to respect and trust adults. Consequently, church camp staff, youth group leaders, and peers all pointed me in the direction of God. My bundle of faith looked like a lovely artichoke, with each Bible story leaf and each answered prayer leaf and each exemplary teacher leaf overlapping one another to form a beautiful artichoke.

Then college hit me, and wham! My neat little artichoke of faith was attacked by all kinds of philosophical arguments which peeled off leaves, one at a time, until I had only a skinny core left. Christianity is not the only way to God. There go some leaves. Who is Jesus? Is He really God? Was He just a good prophet like Buddha and others before Him? There go some other leaves. Was He really born of a virgin? Was He really resurrected? Other leaves fell to the ground. Are all religions different paths up the same mountain of love, Christianity as just one of several paths? Is God a force that does not interact with us personally? Leaves are falling like crazy.

My skinny core of artichoke was comprised of only three core truths. God spoke to me verbally, and therefore is alive and active. God healed the goldfish and therefore does answer prayer. God found my coin purse and therefore can see things we are missing. That is it. That is all I knew; nothing more.

I wanted to know truth. I didn't want to believe what Joe Schmoe said is true or what Jane Crane espouses. I wanted to know truth. Ultimate truth. Desperately! So desperately that I left college after my sophomore year, lived at home while taking a decreased academic load in a nearby university, and wrestled with God to reveal Himself.

I argued with God like no other. "What do You mean when You say in John 8:31–32, 'If you hold to my teaching, you are really my disciples. Then you will know the truth, and the truth will set you free'? God, have You read Exodus and Leviticus? There are a plethora of commandments. I do not feel free. I feel weighed down by all those commandments. How in the world can You say that knowing You will set us free?"

I sometimes felt like I had won the debate. And then, a couple days later, while reading scripture or simply just thinking and reflecting, I suddenly saw the light. "I get it! You mean 'freedom from the bondage of sin.' That is so beautiful. The laws and the commandments point out our sins, but they do not have power to free us from the bondage of sin. Only the Holy Spirit, living within us, can give us victory.

> "You, however, are controlled not by the sinful nature but
> by the Spirit, if the Spirit of God lives in you."
> —Romans 8:9

"OK, God, I get the freedom thing. You can free us from the bondage of sin; from our bad habits and addictions and bad lifestyle choices and bad moods. Jesus applied the verses of Isaiah 61 to Himself as He read this passage aloud to the people in Nazareth (Luke 4:16–19).

> "… He has sent me to bind up the brokenhearted,
> to proclaim freedom for the captives and release
> from darkness for the prisoners, …"
> —Isaiah 61:1

Jesus was bringing soothing salve and relief to those whose hearts have been broken. A broken heart is a hemorrhaging heart. Sometimes people harden their hearts so nothing else can hurt them. But when their heart is hardened, it won't let love go out or love come in. This fortress of hardness that they erect actually walls them in like a captive. Jesus has come to be a bandage to these prisoners; to bind up the heart with a bandage that stops the bleeding, but still allows love to come in and love to pour out. The bandage, unlike the prison wall, promotes healing and is porous so that love can flow in from God and flow out to people. Jesus frees us from our hurts and our bondage to sin.

But what about Jesus? Is He deity or is He just a good prophet? Who is He? That one had me going. The core of my artichoke consisted of what people told me or what I experienced or what beliefs I chose to keep as my own. It was totally me-centered. Now I no longer cared about what I wanted to believe as truth, what I thought sounded intellectually brilliant or philosophically profound. I wanted absolute truth.

The first chapter of John is pretty amazing!

> "In the beginning was the Word,
> and the Word was with God,
> and the Word was God.
> He was with God in the beginning.
> Through him all things were made;
> without him nothing was made
> that has been made ...
> The Word became flesh
> and made his dwelling among us."
>
> —John 1:1–3, 14

So, the Word is Jesus Christ, and Jesus was with God in the creation story, and Jesus is God. He became flesh in the familiar nativity story of the New Testament. But He is part of the Godhead and existed way back in Genesis. Jesus prayed,

> "I have brought you glory on earth
> by completing the work you gave me to do.
> And now, Father, glorify me in your presence
> with the glory I had with you
> before the world began."
>
> —John 17:4–5

There are many other verses that repeat this concept throughout the Bible. The leaf of Jesus being God popped back onto my artichoke. And the idea that He existed at the beginning of creation was a new leaf that sprang out of the artichoke. Was Jesus resurrected? Where is Jesus now?

Paul wrote:

> "For what I received I passed on to you
> as of first importance:
> that Christ died for our sins according
> to the Scriptures, that he was buried,
> that he was raised on the third day according
> to the Scriptures,
> and that he appeared to Peter,
> and then to the Twelve.
> After that, he appeared to more than five hundred of the
> brothers at the same time,
> most of whom are still living,
> though some have fallen asleep.
> Then he appeared to James,
> then to all the apostles,
> and last of all he appeared to me ..."
> —1 Corinthians 15:3–8

Yes, Jesus was resurrected. And He is alive, with God the Father. Before His crucifixion, He told the disciples,

> "I came from the Father and entered the world;
> now I am leaving the world and going
> back to the Father."
> —John 16:28

And He is alive with the Father and is our priest. Hebrews differentiates between our earthly priests and Jesus, who is our priest and who intercedes for us now. He has an active role in our lives now.

> "Now there have been many of those priests,
> since death prevented them from continuing in office;
> but because Jesus lives forever,
> he has a permanent priesthood.
> Therefore he is able to save completely
> those who come to God through him,
> because he always lives to intercede for them."
> —Hebrews 7:23–25

But wait, there are still some amazing contradictions in the Bible. You, God, say in one place that we are saved by grace and not by works. And You say in another place that faith without works is dead. How do you remedy this argument? I thought I had God trapped. It took a few days to get answers to this dilemma, but stick with me.

> "For it is by grace you have been saved, through faith—
> and this not from yourselves,
> it is the gift of God—
> not by works,
> so that no one can boast."
> —Ephesians 2:8–9

"You see that a person is justified
by what he does
and not by faith alone.

As the body without the spirit is dead,
so faith without deeds is dead."
—James 2:24, 26

After a few days of questioning God about this, the light bulb suddenly turned on. "I get it! So, what You are saying, God, is that we cannot earn our salvation by tons of good works. There is no way we can save ourselves. It is a gift You freely give us when we put out faith in You. And when we receive this gift of salvation we have not earned or deserved, we are so full of joy and thanksgiving that it is quite natural for good works to spill out of our lives. If these good works don't spill out of our lives, we probably have not received the free gift of salvation. The two will just go together. But the beautiful part of this promise is that our salvation is not dependent on our works. There is no way any of us can be the perfect people we need to be for the perfect and holy heaven. We all are in need of a Savior and Jesus has come to be that Savior.

"Thank you, God, for answering that question. But how about the concept that 'different religions are different paths up the same mountain of love, and Christianity is just one of those paths?' Is Jesus just another prophet?" Jesus Himself, said He was the Son of God. He told of how He existed before creation and will be our priest forever and intercede for us on a daily basis. When describing Jesus, C.S. Lewis explains we are faced with only three choices:

1) Liar
2) Lunatic
3) Son of God

Some of us want to add a fourth choice such as prophet or good teacher. But since Jesus said He was the Son of God, either He was and is the Son of God, or He is a liar, or He is a crazy person. If He is a liar or a crazy person, then Christianity totally falls apart, for without Christ, Christianity caves in. Other religions can stand, even without their founders. But not Christianity. It is centered on a personal relationship with Christ as well as trusting Him as our Savior. If Christ is the Son of God, then what does He say about the different paths of religion? In John 14:6, Jesus said,

> "I am the way
> and the truth
> and the life.
> No one comes to the Father
> except through me."

In Acts 4:12, we read,

> "Salvation is found in no one else,
> for there is no other name under heaven given to men
> by which we must be saved."

What about people who have never heard about Christ? God is a God of grace. He will judge according to the knowledge people have received. This problem was not my issue. I own a Bible and I have had many opportunities to hear God's Word.

I have only shared a few of the many discussions and arguments from my one year of searching for truth. I started with a leafless artichoke with three me-centered experiences at the core. After memorizing a ton of scriptures, I ended with a core of scriptures from which beliefs and experiences became petals. This new artichoke of faith, with scriptures as its core, has stood the test of time during the good seasons of my life as well as the dark seasons. I can't wait to share with you some of those unbelievable stories.

So what does your artichoke of faith look like? What are the core beliefs for you and on whom are they based? Are they springing out of your own philosophical constructs? Who is at the center of your artichoke, you or God? Do you have questions? Seek truth, and God will help you find it. Life is full of questions, and we never arrive with a perfect artichoke of faith. Leaves continue to grow.

Chapter 4

INCOMPREHENSIBLE

GOD IS INCOMPREHENSIBLY big. Isn't that great! We can't contain Him within a statue; we can't comprehend His ways, for His ways are not our ways and His thoughts are not our thoughts. He is in control of the universe, and that is huge.

Let's think about the universe. Alpha Centauri is considered to be the closest star to our sun. Our sun and Alpha Centauri are next-door neighbors! So how close are these two neighbors? This blows our minds. They are 4.3 light years apart! You're kidding me. Oh my goodness! Let me try to get my mind wrapped around this. A light year is the distance light travels in one year. I am still not comprehending. Slow down.

So how far does light travel in a second? I live in Washington State, and we have the Space Needle in Seattle. Let's pretend we are standing a few feet away from the Space Needle when lightning strikes. We see the lightning and hear thunder all at the same time. Now, let's walk a mile away from the Space Needle. Lightning strikes the needle once again. This time we see the lightning, and five seconds later we hear the thunder. What happened? The sound travels more slowly than the light. So, in one second of time, how far does light travel? Even though light from the Space Needle travels in a straight line, let's pretend the light follows the curvature of Earth. If it curved around the surface of the earth, in one second of time, would it go halfway across the United States? Or, in one second of time, would it go clear across the United States? In one second of time, would it get as far as halfway around the earth? How far would it go?

Some of you are way ahead of me, but have patience, I am catching up. The light, in one second of time, would go a distance equal to encircling the entire earth six and one half times. If we were floating out in space a straight line distance equal to six and a half earth circumferences away from the Space Needle, lightning could strike the Space Needle and one second later we would see the flash. Thunder, on the other hand, would take ten days to reach us.

That is incredible! I know the mathematical numbers make sense when one takes the velocity of light and circumference of the earth into consideration, but picturing the light traveling a straight line distance outward from the Space Needle equaling the distance of encircling the earth six and a half times in one second is quite another challenge.

I picked up a world globe and tried to rotate my finger around the globe six and a half times in one second. I could not even do that. Imagining how far light goes in one second of time is nearly incomprehensible.

Now try imagining how far light goes in 4.3 years. And that is the distance to our nearest star beyond our own sun. If, on the day you were born, someone carried you out to the nighttime sky where you could gaze at the stars, you would see light from the nearest star that started its journey to you 4.3 years before you were born. If you feel like you are comprehending, then you are not comprehending. How can anyone imagine such distances? Pause. Gasp for air.

Too often I visualize God as a superman, who is like us, but with only a little more power and a little more knowledge. I forget that He is the Creator of this huge universe; He is bigger than the universe He created. I stuff Him in a box and limit His powers. However, the more I reflect on the magnitude of His created universe, the bigger He becomes in my thinking, and the better I am able to trust my life into His loving care.

When we look up into the sky, we see all the stars from our own Milky Way galaxy. Our galaxy is shaped like a giant pancake with Earth about midway between the center of our galaxy and the rim on our galaxy. The Milky Way stars we see in the irregular ribbon of light spanning across our skies are stars on the rim of the pancake. This lovely galaxy pancake is about 10,000 light years in thickness at the center, tapers off toward the rim, and has a diameter with a distance of about 100,000 light years. No easy pancake to flip!

When we look up at the stars from our city streets, we see a countable number of stars. But when we pitch a tent on a desert in Mexico, the star-studded canopy makes us speechless. Add an orbiting Hubble space telescope and other discoveries of science, and we face a hundred billion or more stars whirling within our galactic system.

If your brain is not whirling almost into a comatose state, consider that all the stars we see with our naked eye are stars only in our own galaxy. In addition to the hundred billion or more stars in our galaxy, there are hundreds of billions of galaxies in the universe. I don't know about you, but I am hyperventilating. Truly I can agree with the psalmist who wrote:

"The heavens declare the glory of God."

—Psalm 19:1

Now, if we have any brain cells still functioning, let's step away from the telescope and gaze into a microscope. When I was in the seventh grade, my two-dimensional drawings of cells looked like fried eggs, where the yolk was the nucleus, containing the protons and neutrons. The egg white was the empty space through which electrons darted around. The fundamental particles of matter were protons, neutrons, and electrons. Today we are told that the fundamental particles of matter include quarks, leptons, and their antiparticles. Our old friend the proton is composed of two up quarks and one down quark. Did I mention colors? The quarks come in red, blue, or green. But the antiquarks come in colors of antired, antiblue, and antigreen. And when a quark and an antiquark collide, they annihilate each other. I want my next car to be antiblue. If I could park next to a blue car, we could become invisible. No-fault insurance will have to cover collisions from invisible cars. I did not back into a tree; a "quarky" blue car rammed into me from out of nowhere!

Hold on! It gets even more complicated. The fried-egg cell has now turned into a sophisticated factory. It is amazing! The first time I watched a computer simulation of the inner workings of a human cell, my brain felt like a fried egg. Thirteen feet of DNA is packed into a nucleus that has a diameter of about 0.005 millimeters. And the microscopic strand of DNA has three billion bits of information, called base pairs, which make up a person's genetic alphabet. One little spelling mistake can cause serious diseases. The message in the DNA tells every other part of the cell how to do its work. And the work looks like a complicated, highly sophisticated factory.

So, if you feel like having a brain explosion, choose to look through either a telescope or a microscope. Marveling over the vastness of the universe and the comparative smallness of our own bodies, coupled with reveling over the incredible complexities and divine design in our bodies, tosses our mind in a quandary. Where does man fit in relationship to God? How important are we to God?

One of my favorite passages in the Bible is Psalm 139. The first four verses impress upon me how He knows and loves each one of us.

> "O LORD, you have searched me and you know me.
> You know when I sit and when I rise;
> you perceive my thoughts from afar.
> You discern my going out and my lying down;
> you are familiar with all my ways.
> Before a word is on my tongue
> you know it completely, O LORD."

He knows us better than we know ourselves, because He created us. He knows our thoughts and what we are going to say before we say it. He is familiar with our quirky personalities, and yet, He loves us a thousand times more than anyone loves us, because He is God. We are "fearfully and wonderfully made." In verses 17 and 18, the psalm continues:

"How precious to me are your thoughts, O God!
How vast is the sum of them!
Were I to count them,
they would outnumber the grains of sand.
When I awake,
I am still with you."

God is with us all the time. He will never leave or forsake us. In essence, our picture is on God's refrigerator door.

We can glibly spout out that God is all-knowing (omniscient), present everywhere at the same time (omnipresent), and all-powerful (omnipotent) without comprehending His potential impact on our lives.

Consider God's omniscience. If He is really omniscient, then He can help us with learning Hebrew or studying microbiology or managing children. He knows the answers for any test that has been written and He knows the contents of every book. He knows what has yet to be discovered and what will never be discovered. We can come to Him with our questions and frustrations, for He has answers. We can trust Him with our lives, because He is all-knowing, all-present, all-powerful, all-holy, and all-loving. He is our loving Heavenly Father. Glory hallelujah!

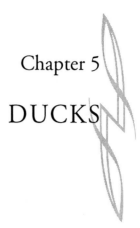

Chapter 5

DUCKS

GOD'S OMNISCIENCE AND my ineptness collided on Monday, November 2, 1969, in my physics class.

My story actually starts back in the summer of 1969, when I was engaged for only seven days before we broke off the relationship. With my heart shattered into pieces, I resolved that it would be a long time before I would let myself fall in love again; a long time indeed. To guard against the foolishness of love, I made up rules for myself. First of all, I stopped teaching and enrolled in the master's program for physics majors at the University of Washington. Being surrounded by such exciting men, I would not have to fall in love with them to enjoy their conversations. Secondly, I decided that lunch dates or coffee dates would be permissible as long as I never went out more than once with any person. The plan almost worked.

Dave wasn't in my physics classes, and I forgot to make up rules for folk dancing. We met for a dinner date, and then … How do I explain this? He brought up some interesting questions in our conversation, which I wanted to continue exploring. One dinner date was just not long enough. But I also did not want to violate my one-date rule. What was I to do? Reason came to my rescue! He was scheduled to leave by November to serve in the army in the Vietnam War. It would be impossible for me to fall in love with him in only two and a half months. Therefore, he could be an exception to my one-date rule. He was a totally safe person.

Interesting questions multiplied while physics problems escalated. In the middle of this cranial battlefield, my heart started doing those little flip-flops. Fearing those emotions of love, I carefully crafted a letter to end our relationship. I wrote as gently as possible, knowing he was a sensitive person whom I did not want to totally crush. Apparently, I was quite gentle, for he thought it was a love letter. I prayed God would take away my emotions of love. That didn't work. "God, I have lost my confidence in Your taking away my emotions of love. But I have total confidence that You can make him not like me." God must have just laughed.

A bouquet of roses later, I knelt down on the floor and confessed to God, "When he comes back from Vietnam, and if he asks me to marry him, I am going to say yes." To confirm my decision, I walked from my boardinghouse down to the University District jewelry stores.

Ring shopping is tricky business. I didn't want to buy anything; I just wanted to look. As I peered around a couple to look at some rings, a clerk jumped in front of me with,

"May I help you?"

"Oh, yes, I am looking for a watch."

He pointed over his shoulder to where the watches were. I

dutifully followed and he left me alone. My "shopping" resulted in gazing at rings, several feet away, while standing in the watch section. Not easily deterred, I reminded myself that this was not the only ring shop in the district. However, I had much the same experience at the second ring shop. As long as I stayed with watches, clerks would leave me alone. Since Dave and I had not even breathed the word "marriage," ring gazing was totally absurd. Or so I thought. It turns out that Dave was doing the same thing, at the same time, only thirty miles away.

After working his nursing shift at Good Samaritan Hospital, he was so excited to be leaving for his visit with me in Seattle that he made a practice of bounding down the hospital stairs by leaping from landing to landing without hitting the stair steps in between the landings. His daily aerodynamics was adversely affected when a pebble on one of the landings caused his launching foot to slip backwards, altering his trajectory so that he landed on his shoulder rather than on his feet. Upon hearing this story, one of his wise patients suggested marriage. Thus, Dave was visiting ring shops in Tacoma on the same day I was venturing through jewelry stores in Seattle.

In the evening of our secret ring-shopping day, we ordered Hefty Burgers from Herfy's Drive-In. Neither of us had confided our secret ring-shopping excursions. Dave said,

"There is something I want to tell you; no, ask you; uh, well, never mind." And we continued to munch on our burgers. Minutes later, with renewed courage, he again remarked,

"There is something I want to ask you. No, forget it."
My curiosity was definitely aroused. At the conclusion of our burger dining, he asked,

"Do you want me to take you back to the boardinghouse so you can study for your big physics exam, or, uh, do you want to go to Green Lake to look at the ducks?"

He held his breath while various thoughts screamed through my head. There was something he had on his mind. What was that all about? But then, I did have a huge test looming in front of me. The physics class was really hard, and I knew I needed to study practically nonstop until the test on Monday morning. But those Green Lake ducks are pretty special.

"I want to go to Green Lake and look at the ducks."

Those ducks changed my life! We drove to Green Lake, and yes, all you people who are concocting what we really did, you are wrong. We did look at the ducks. Yes, we did. And then, my courageous Dave blurted it out. With no preambles, he looked at me and asked,

"Will you marry me?"

Before I could answer, he turned swiftly around, grabbed the steering wheel, and stared out the windshield. This left me looking at his right ear when I replied, before he had even left for Vietnam,

"Yes, I will."

From that moment on we turned into crazy people.

The next day, Friday, as I was walking across campus, the sun was brilliantly yellow, the grass an emerald green, and the birds were singing more than ever. I was crying with tears of joy. Like I said, we were crazy people. On Saturday we spent several hours between his two favorite ring stores in Tacoma, debating between two rings, one in each store. Back and forth we flew in what would become our habitual indecisive state when making important decisions. We finally settled on the perfect ring. Sunday afternoon I returned to my boardinghouse to begin studying for the all-important test.

This story is only the preamble to the real story I want to tell you. I can't wait to get it out and my fingers are flying and my computer keys are scrambling around as I type Hebrew, or whatever, instead of English. (I don't know Hebrew, in case anybody out there falsely surmises I have linguistic talents.)

As I settled down to study physics, my sparkling ring got in the way. The physics seemed so dry and so boring. I felt for the first time in my life that I might be able to read poetry and understand it. But this physics was arid dry. My heart was racing, my mind was poetic, and the equations were not registering. I tried to get serious, but it was a losing battle. I decided to go to bed early, get up super early, and study like crazy.

Even though I was in a master's level of physics, I am not a gifted physicist. The class was exceptionally difficult for me. The professor did not teach sequentially from our textbook. So, there were times I had no idea of whether he was talking about mechanical physics, electromagnetism, optics, or nuclear physics. I did not know where in the index I could turn for more information. He used mathematical operators I had never seen before. It was literally like another language to me. It never occurred to me that I could drop the course. Because I sat in the second row from the front, I did not observe until much too late that about one-third of the class had dropped the course. Fortunately for me, I sat next to Mr. Genius. I wish I could remember his name, so I could officially give him credit. But Mr. Genius was not just super smart, he was also super humble. I madly took notes like everyone else in the class, while Mr. Genius absorbed all the professor expounded without needing to copy everything down. I knew whenever the professor made a mistake, because Mr. Genius nervously shifted in his chair, flexed his legs, and stiffened up as he hoped the professor would catch the mistake. After a time, if the mistake went unnoticed, Mr. Genius courageously raised his hand and said something like,

"I think there might be a mistake in the fourth row down of the second column on the board." And sure enough, he was always right. The professor went back and erased spots here and there and made appropriate corrections as the rest of us crossed out our notes in ink and tried to duplicate the corrections.

Other times the professor realized his mistake without the help of Mr. Genius. At those times, Mr. Genius let out a big sigh of relief. Many times after class I asked Mr. Genius where in our textbook I could find more information about the class presentation. He was unbelievably kind and helpful. If I had the brain of Mr. Genius I would have been spouting out corrections right away. Maybe that is why God reserved the brains for Mr. Genius.

In case you haven't already figured this out, I was barely making it grade-wise in this class. I had fully intended to study about thirty hours for the Monday test. I did get up around four a.m. on Monday to resume studying, but by 9:30 a.m. I had not even finished reading the chapter. There were a ton of problems I needed to practice once the reading was completed. This was not good. The thought of faking a serious illness never entered my mind. Instead, I reasoned,

"I will go to the professor, show him my ring, tell him this is a once-in-a-lifetime experience, and ask if he could give me one more day to study for the test."

Great plan. No, maybe a stupid plan. I did carry through on my part, and my professor just laughed at me in front of the

46

five other students who were in his office with questions they wanted answered before taking the test. Retreating back to our classroom, I stood outside the door, reading the last paragraph of the chapter. I had done no problems. Not good.

Tests were handed out. I turned mine over upside down on my desk and prayed a simple prayer: "Dear Lord, I do not deserve to pass this test, because I have not studied. I pray that You will pull out of my mind anything that I might know. Thank you, Jesus. Amen." I turned over the test and discovered there was a total of four problems with an hour to work them. I was not going to just draw pictures for an hour, mainly because my artistic skills have not advanced beyond first-grade stick pictures. The first problem was hard. I tried doing what I could do. The second and third ones made more sense. The fourth was a mystery. I did what I could do.

After class I joined another student for a walk to Herfy's. Those Hefty Burgers were the best! We both hoped that we had earned a D on the test.

On the day of reckoning, I heard students behind me comparing their scores. Grades must have been raw scores and not percentages, for they were sharing scores in the twenties and thirties. I waited in dread for my paper. My score was a 63 and Mr. Genius scored only 4 points higher than I. Really and truly! This made no sense to me!!

As the professor explained problem one, I did not understand how he went from one of the middle steps to the next step. He explained his rationale, but I didn't comprehend what he was saying. But when I looked at my paper, I had the exact thing written on my own paper. I started to panic. I need to know how I did this and why I did this. It is on my paper and I don't get it. He then went on to problems two and three, which made more sense to me. But when he discussed problem four, I again ran into a place in his explanation that made no sense. And again, like problem one, my steps on my paper matched what he had written on the board. I was nearly shaking at this point. I pushed the paper as far away from myself as possible and withdrew from it as if it were "holy paper." I felt like God had written my paper.

I have a list of questions I want to ask God when I get to heaven. But I fear I won't be able to take the list with me and I might forget what I want to ask. If only I could make a one-day visit to heaven and then come back again. I would like to hear God's side of the story. I learned from that experience two things. First of all, I learned God knows everything about everything. There is no question in physics or math or biology or art or history or geology or languages for which He does not know the answer. And secondly, when we go to Him for help, He does hear and answer our prayers.

To set the record straight, the physics test is the only test I ever took where I felt like God wrote it. He is not a Santa Claus who allows us to play in the park so He can take our tests. But after having more than one heartbreaking relationship crash, I felt like His stamp of approval was on my relationship with Dave. And in later years when we went through dark times in our marriage, the stamp-of-approval physics test kept my eyes on the Lord and gave me encouragement.

> His ways are not our ways!
> He is God of the impossible!
> (Isaiah 55:8 and Luke 18:27)

Chapter 6

ASK

REMINDING ME THAT I can turn to God for help with physics changed the way I tackled my academics. While taking an independent study astronomy course, I ran into a question which I labored over for an hour with no answers. I was a busy wife and mom plus full-time teacher. I did not have time to spend an hour of writing nothing. I got angry at this good-for-nothing astronomy book and the time the course was taking. Stomping out of the room, I found some packaged macaroni and cheese, which would be perfect for a quick lunch. Vigorously stirring the pot, my anger fumed over the book's ineptness in answering questions. I was stuck. I needed to get on with my life, but the perplexing question had my wheels spinning, and was getting me nowhere.

Eventually, I turned to God, who truly knows everything. I told Him I did not have time for non-productivity and that He knew the answers and I needed to know the answer. "God, I'm still a bit angry with the book and the questions, and I am not sure I can listen to You just yet." It took a while for my anger to subside. "OK Lord, I think I have a teachable heart." Returning to the study, I settled down into our comfy computer chair and took a couple of deep breaths. "Heavenly Father, I pray You will show me the answer to the astronomy question. My mind has run into a dead end, and I need to get the question answered so I can return to my other responsibilities of being a wife and mother and schoolteacher. Please help me."

Placing my hands lightly on the computer keyboard, I held them motionless, and waited. A thought appeared in my mind. "Well, that is only one sentence, but I guess I can write that one sentence." I did. Then another sentence came. And then, you guessed it. I kept writing and the answer just flowed. It was an intense and amazing hour. Paragraphs later, I pushed back in my chair and said, "Thank you, thank you, thank you, God."

Through the years, I have continued to learn more about partnering up with God over all kinds of challenges. I characteristically find myself approaching the panic level, back away, call upon God, and marvel over how He carries me through the situation.

Calculus was a great schoolmaster for teaching me to trust and lean upon God. When I was given a chance to teach Advanced Placement Calculus at my high school, I wanted to jump at the opportunity. But two things stood in my way. I was afraid my unskilled teaching might ruin the good reputation of our student performance on the Advanced Placement national test. And I knew the calculus I had learned thirty years earlier was not the current calculus being taught. Who would coach me?

People encouraged me to take the plunge and I dove into calculus. God was my instructor as I prayed my way through the problems and teaching preparations. What a year of faith that was! I remember walking into the classroom one day with three of my students at the board discussing how to work a certain problem. It was a complicated one to explain. As I walked into the classroom, all eyes, riveted on me, asked for an explanation. It was the same problem I had struggled with only minutes before the class without successfully resolving. I took a deep breath, and out came an explanation that surprised me and calmed everyone down. "Thank you, God. That came more from You than from me."

Another time I was trying to make sense out of a theorem that I would teach in a couple days. There was one step in the theorem that made no sense. I labored over that theorem for a couple hours. Frustration built, driving me once again to the Master Teacher. I paced the floor as I poured out my heart. "Heavenly Father, I don't understand this theorem. You understand it. Please show me what I am missing." I prayed until I felt like God truly heard me. I sat down again with the same page before me. "So You mean, God, that if I assume this other truth, that this step leads into this step, which goes … But when I was working it before, I started with this other truth that sprang out of … that would take me to … Why didn't my truth work? Wait … I think I see what You might be saying …" Yes, it took a half hour of communication like this with God, but it did eventually make sense. I pushed back my chair, relieved, and sighed, "Thank you, thank you, thank you, God."

When we get tangled up in our problems, why doesn't God just reach down, without our asking, and tweak our brains a little until things make sense? Why do we need to ask Him for help? I don't know. But when we fall on our knees, pour out our needs, and ask for His help, great things happen. Sometimes, in my teaching, certain concepts did not make sense to my students. I tried using different words, drawing illustrations, talking more slowly … nothing seemed to help. At the end of my creativity, I stopped and prayed with the class that God, our mighty teacher, would help us. We then sat in silence until I came up with new words or, as often happened, a student came up with an explanation that cleared up all the confusion.

This "asking" principle is a big mystery to me. Sometimes we receive surprises with no previous asking. Early in our marriage, we moved from being dormitory parents to living in our own home, which we purchased for $5,000. Suffice it to say, the house did not make it onto the cover page of *House Beautiful* magazine. Dave attended college and our food budget was a bit slim. One day two big paper bags packed with food appeared on our front porch. Friends told us they needed to "clean out their freezer" before going on a trip. Some items in those sacks testified to a recent cleaning out of the supermarket. And then a few weeks later we agreed that purchasing a Christmas tree would not happen. A few nights later, our neighbor, whom we hardly knew, surprised us with what he termed "an extra tree." We praise God for these special people and their gifts of love. We were not starving to death and we could certainly survive Christmas without a tree, but God lavishly gave us gifts through wonderful friends, without our asking.

Other times God waits for us to ask. The story that has spoken volumes to me occurred when I was in the fifth grade. I had an official note that needed to be delivered to a student in another class. Instead of giving the note to the teacher, who would, in turn, hand it to the student, I blatantly walked into the classroom and handed it to the student without going through the teacher. The teacher called me aside, in front of the class, and quietly explained to me that I should have given him the note first. I was humiliated and felt like I had committed the world's worst sin. Every night before going to sleep, I relived this horrible day. And when I awoke in the morning, I replayed the wrong I committed in that classroom. This incident tormented me for about a month. Finally, I turned to God in prayer, and simply said, "Forgive me for not giving the note to the teacher." That is all I said. I was totally unprepared for God's answer. He forgave me by completely lifting all the weight of my guilt. I felt light and free. It was amazing. I never returned to reliving the torment. I learned the power of asking. God could have removed the guilt when He saw the torment I suffered. But He didn't. He waited until I asked for His forgiveness. And then He lavishly answered my prayer.

In my first year of teaching, I had a student in my class who I really did not like. I prayed one night that God would give me love for this girl, because it was hard teaching a class if I did not feel love for every student. I uttered my prayer one time and then basically forgot about it. Three days later, I was standing in front of the class, and I suddenly felt overwhelming emotions of love toward this girl. It was amazing. And then I remembered the prayer. God answered that prayer so well that to this day, by the grace of God, I cannot remember what it was that made me not like the student. I was not able to love that precious girl on my own efforts, but through Christ's work I couldn't keep from loving her! The Holy Spirit changes our hearts when we can't. However, He does not force Himself into our life, but often waits until we ask.

This causes me to question, "How much do we not receive because we don't ask?"

I remember a rather embarrassing time of experiencing Holy Spirit fruit as the result of asking for God's intervention. I was a young mom with my fifteen-month-old daughter hospitalized for cleft palate surgery. With basically no roof in Stacey's mouth, I could see her nasal passages when I looked inside her mouth. Without a roof for her tongue to press against, she was unable to talk clearly. Until a week after surgery, I did not know that Stacey had been talking in complete sentences. Since her words sounded like babble, I thought she was just making noises.

Getting back to my story: little Stacey was in the hospital recovering from surgery. One morning of her recovery, I slipped away from the hospital for two hours to attend a Bible study leadership meeting, where we were told to put Ps and Ts in our Bible study margins to help us when leading our group discussions. The Ps pertained to number of people to call on and the Ts had something to do with the time allotted to each question. I don't remember the details. All I remember is that my margins were already filled up with my own comments that I considered very important, and now I was being told to add ridiculous Ps and Ts in places where I did not have room for such useless information. I questioned the policy and was told to "just do it." Now that aroused my wrath. The more I thought about it, the angrier I got. Yes, I may have been slightly fatigued over Stacey's surgery, but nevertheless, my anger took off on its own cyclone, intensifying as I drove to the hospital. I contrived an angry letter I was going to spew out to the leader of this whole mess with the Ps and Ts. By the time I arrived at the hospital, I was ready to spear anyone who mentioned anything about Ps and Ts. I was ready for battle.

However, as I approached the hospital rotating doors, I realized that my daughter on the second floor did not need an angry mom. She was in desperate need of a compassionate, caring mom. Let's focus on the nature of anger, for a moment. When

I am angry, really angry, do I want to be rid of my anger? No! I want to be angrier! But anger leaves no room for compassion. As I pushed against the revolving door, I prayed, "Lord, take this anger away." By the time I had completed the half circle of rotation, my anger was totally gone. No anger! Gone! And in its place I felt total peace … the peace that relaxes your entire body. I have never in my whole life before this time or even after this time experienced such a rapid evaporation of flaming anger. It must have taken about two seconds max. I am telling you, the peace I received did not originate from my heart. It came directly from God. And in that moment, God gave my daughter a mom full of peace and compassion.

The story makes me laugh. Have you ever heard of anyone getting so angry over two letters of the alphabet? Anyway, the anger never returned for the Ps and Ts. I wrote them as required, but, I must confess, I wrote them with very tiny letters!

All of this to say, we have an omniscient God who impacts our lives. His grace flows abundantly into our lives if we are open to receive. Sometimes we don't receive, because we don't ask. Sometimes we receive even when we don't ask. Sometimes we receive so much more than we dare to ask.

We rejoice, because we have a loving Heavenly Father who delights in lavishly pouring His grace upon us.

> "Delight yourself in the Lord and he will give you the
> desires of your heart."
>
> —Psalm 37:4

Chapter 7

BEYOND
EXPECTATIONS

IF GOD IS busy running the universe and prioritizing the millions of prayer requests that come His way, surely He does not have time to hear me talk about my sore foot or my bad mood. Wrong! I cannot explain God. All I can say is that He is Master of doing the unexpected.

With our family of six stuffed into our van along with our dog and cat, and towing a homemade trailer piled high with belongings, we moved from Texas to Washington State. In the rural countryside of New Mexico, our van tire went flat. I suggested we pull into a gas station and seek help. My burly husband did not appreciate that comment. Not wanting to be onstage in front of curious onlookers, he chose to turn down an obscure little street where he could take his time with the car surgery. He tried jacking up the car with his car jack, but the heavy trailer worked against him. His only hope was to unhook the trailer and try again. It was hot, we were tired, and the job looked daunting. Just then, an old man with a long, straggly beard walked out from behind his home and hobbled over to us, offering his hydraulic jack, which would not require unhooking the trailer. What a gift! How in the world did we manage to park our car in front of a home where a generous man with a hydraulic jack resided? Why did we turn down that particular street and park in front of that particular house? Thank you, God. Your grace is amazing.

And then there were the baby shoes. I know. Children in many countries run around in bare feet all the time. Shoes are not always a necessity. And certainly, in our nicely carpeted churches, children do not need to be wearing shoes. But, I must confess, I did not want Bryna to be the only child in the nursery without shoes. Not for her sake, but for my own personal pride.

What kind of a mother loses her child's only pair of shoes? That would be me. So I ran around in a hysterical fit of panic, searching everywhere for the shoes, as time ticked away. In desperation, I finally resorted to prayer. Why am I so slow to pray? And when I pray, I so often have so little faith that God will answer. I am a slow learner when it comes to prayer. "Dear Lord Jesus, You have eyes that see everything. You can see those shoes right now. You know where they are. I do not know where they are. Please lead me to the shoes. I pray in Jesus' name. Amen."

That was the prayer. I sat and waited. And then I walked straight into the bathroom, opened up the clothes hamper, and pulled out the entire bin of clothes. At the bottom of the hamper, lo and behold, you guessed it! The baby shoes!

I never remembered doing anything that would cause those shoes to land at the bottom of the clothes hamper. I do not know how they found their way down through the clothes. And after I prayed, the first place I looked was in the hamper. Go figure!

The same thing happened with a test I had written. Needing to pick up my two younger children from their child care, I frantically searched my desk for the test I had carefully written and needed to duplicate for class the next day. I distinctly remembered slipping it in the front of the papers of my top left-hand desk drawer. I even remember checking on it throughout the day. But now, it was gone. I looked through various folders in the file cabinet across the room. I searched all the drawers in my desk. It was gone! Totally gone! It couldn't be gone. It had to be somewhere. I frantically ran downstairs to call my friend and let her know I would be picking up my children as soon as I could find the test. I finally collapsed in my big wooden teacher chair, and prayed,

"Dear God, You know where that test is. I do not know where it is. Please Lord Jesus, I need to find it. Show me where it is. In Your precious name I pray. Amen." And then I sat in the big chair with my arms stretched out over my desk. I tried to make my mind blank of all my thoughts so I could receive what God might be saying. I waited. Motionless. My right hand reached up, took out a folder from a rack on my desk, opened it, and there it was! I couldn't believe it! And then I remembered. Ah, yes. I remembered checking on that test, which was in the top drawer of my desk, and discovering that it was slightly wrinkled from the numerous times I opened the drawer. So, I had removed it from the drawer and placed it in a folder in my rack. Strange how my mind could only remember the drawer move and totally forgot the folder move.

I jumped up and shouted, "Thank you, thank you, thank you, God." I danced and shouted and ran to the copy machine. Grabbing my purse, I ran to get my children. But, wait a minute. Oh my goodness, where were my keys? "No, God! Not again!

This can't be." This time my frantic search lasted only a couple minutes until I returned back to the big chair, hands outstretched over my desk, and prayed once again.

"Dear God, here we go again. You see my keys. I do not see them. You know where they are. I desperately need to find them. I am going to sit here and wait until You can show me where they are. I pray this in Jesus' holy name. Amen."

I opened my eyes and sat. I quietly surveyed my surroundings, and then, over there, on top of the file cabinet where I had torn through all the folders, there were my keys innocently resting in plain view.

Was God laughing? I was! Life can be crazy funny!!

What a privilege we have to enter into God's throne room at any time and in any place. What a joy when God answers prayers over mundane baby shoes and missing papers. We don't have to wait in a room for non-emergency prayers. We are not stuck on call waiting. We are not shuffled down to the secretary to schedule an interview with God or with some saint who died two hundred years ago. We are not told that God is too busy to help us. We are not just allowed to visit with God; we are invited into His presence. He cares about us and about the details of our lives, and He lavishly pours out His grace.

Sometimes God's grace comes to us in a quiet voice, speaking to our innermost self. We don't ask for it, we aren't even thinking of God, and lo and behold, He speaks in our minds. One occasion stands out in my mind.

I was standing in line, waiting for my turn to pay for family pictures, which I had ordered. The line was moving slowly, but I was getting close, when suddenly, feeling an urgency to go home, I left my place in line.

A month earlier, one of my daughters came home from school with four male baby hamsters. We had never had hamsters, and I dubiously asked how they knew they were all male. I got some answer like, "The teacher said so. They were definitely all males."

Seventeen babies later, we discovered two were females. And those two gave birth to their brood on the same day and in the same cage while I was away choosing pictures. Apparently, when too many babies occupy too little space, the adult hamsters begin eating their young.

As I drove up to our house, Stacey cried out, traumatized, from the porch,

"Mom, hurry. Do something!"

Her face was stricken with panic. She was totally traumatized. The babies were pink little things with no hair and they were squealing as they were being eaten. Stacey couldn't stand touching them and couldn't stand hearing the screams. Being the oldest sibling around, she felt responsibility to do something, and instead suffered rescue paralysis. Teryl had run into my bedroom and was crying. Bryna had run off into the woods. And I was supposed to know what to do.

Yes, the Lord did call me out of the picture line for a reason. For all of you pet lovers, we saved thirteen of the babies by separating them into different cages. Two days later, however, one of the mothers disappeared. I eventually discovered the new nest she had made in my evening coat, where she made a six-inch hole in the armpit. She turned up a couple weeks later sniffing Stacey's hand one night while Stacey was asleep in bed. Yes, we all woke up to Stacey's screams. Meanwhile, the missing mother's babies were orphans. Our attempt at feeding them with an eyedropper turned out to be a milk shower over their entire bodies, leaving them not only hungry, but cold and wet. Our solution to this problem was to stir up the nine babies of the remaining mother, add our four orphans to the box, and hope the mother could not count. It worked. The mom was bad at arithmetic and they lived.

In His grace, the Lord called me out of the picture line and allowed me to comfort my children and restore peace in the chaotic hamster world. I don't claim any special spiritual sensitivity giftings. God simply nudged me, by His grace, in the direction I needed to go.

Sometimes God's grace shows up in our weaknesses. When the apostle Paul pleaded to have God remove his thorn in the flesh, God, refusing his request, replied, "My grace is sufficient for you, for my power is made perfect in weakness" (2 Corinthians 12:9).

God's power has been manifested through my migraine headaches. I have made many trips to emergency rooms in order to stop the vomiting stage of the migraine, while medications added their own drama of side effects, some of which became life threatening. However, God's power in my weakest moments has been evident to me and to others who have assisted me during the migraine episodes.

After a day of teaching, one rather humorous migraine attack escalated in going-home traffic. All the feeder roads to the famous Narrows Bridge characteristically jammed up with drivers trying to beat the system of waiting one's turn. My pounding headache joined forces with my tumultuous stomach, and despite my denial, wreaked havoc. My mind was saying, "I'll get home soon, lie down, and all will be well." But the nausea intensified. And those salivary glands in my mouth started the little three-second preliminary that comes right before the big vomiting. I saw myself, dressed up in my pretty navy-blue dress with the white crocheted collar, stopping my lane of traffic while I jumped out of the car to vomit in front of everyone I most likely would see again in a supermarket on the other side of the bridge. Not a pretty picture. "No, God, not now. Please. Let me get across the bridge and then I can pull over and throw up."

The salivary glands stopped salivating. That is a miracle! Once those glands start working, there is no stopping! They stopped! I crept across the bridge and noted a place on the other side of the bridge where I could pull over. However, my throw-up warning glands were quiet. I cautiously ventured forth, always looking for a place to pull over. I continued driving home, watching for places to pull off the road and noting that I was getting closer and closer to home. Twenty minutes later I arrived in my driveway and managed to get into the bathroom before the inevitable happened. I thank God for saving me from making a scene on the Narrows Bridge and for His care in driving home. He cares about the details of our lives and gives us His grace when we need it.

Another migraine hit me hard during pregnancy when medications were severely limited. I phoned a lady in our church for prayer support, and miraculously, twenty minutes later, with no medications, my headache totally lifted. Migraines don't just evaporate; but that one did. Thank you, Jesus!

Another migraine hit in Mexico, where high school students poured out prayers for me, averting emergency room hospitalization. In the jungles of Ecuador, I fell victim to still another debilitating migraine along with a foodborne illness. A prayer team of women reached through my mosquito netting, massaged my legs, and prayed for me in Spanish. Even though I did not understand any of their words, I felt the power of their prayers. My responses in my limited Spanish were, "Gracias, gracias." "Mucho gracias." "Mucho mucho gracias." I felt bathed in their gentleness and kindness. I later learned I should be saying "muchas" instead of "mucho." The Holy Spirit was our translator!

When we are at our weakest, God is at His strongest, ministering to us in mysterious and unpredictable ways. He gives us His grace when we need it, and not a moment before.

Chapter 8

THE LIST

A S FIRST GRADERS, Lorrie and I were walking with the traffic light and talking while crossing the four-lane highway on our way home from school. We had just passed the halfway mark when we suddenly spotted the car approaching the intersection. I jumped backwards, Lorrie ran forward, and the car sped through right between us. The wind from the moving car nearly knocked me down. The driver sped through, not slowing down and maybe not even seeing us. How did we remain unscathed?

Infant Stacey was mastering her art of sitting. She was sitting about a foot away from the sharp corner of the door jamb. Suddenly she lost her balance and flew backwards. The wooden framework had a sharp edge. She was accelerating backwards, only about an inch from hitting the edge, when all of a sudden she fell sideways. Never have I seen anyone fall in an "L" shape. It violates Newton's first law of motion: an object continues in its state of uniform motion in a straight line, unless it is acted upon by an unbalanced force. It looked like a hand must have pushed her to the side just before her head was about to crack into the sharp edge. I did not see the hand, but I saw the result of another force entering into the scene. Transfixed in one spot, I felt like there should be an orchestra playing a Hallelujah chorus. Something amazing just happened. I saw the effects of something in the unseen world. Stacey rolled onto her tummy and was oblivious to the horrible accident she escaped.

Toddler Bryna insisted on going up the ladder of the big slide. Teryl, two years older, led the way. I held my hands around independent Bryna without touching her as she confidently climbed the steps. When Teryl reached the top, she took one look at the long, slick slide and announced, "I am not going down."

I took my eyes off Bryna and looked up at Teryl. "You have to go down, because here comes Bryna." Bryna had been standing at about my shoulder when I turned from Teryl and saw Bryna falling headfirst toward the cement landing. She was about one foot from hitting the ground when I saw her and then, crash! Why wasn't she crying? Why wasn't her head bleeding? I grabbed Teryl and we ran to a friend's house close by the park. We examined her pupils, and they looked good. She was thirsty. Is that a good sign or a bad sign? Afraid to give her water, we let her sip a small amount. We waited for something horrible to happen—seizures; suddenly falling asleep; coma. But nothing happened. After an hour or so of waiting and watching, I gathered up my two children and headed home. Why did a bruise never show up on her head? Why no headaches or head sores? What happened? I saw her dive headfirst into the cement.

Such incidents demand answers. Two girls in the middle of the third lane should have been run over by the car racing through a red light. What prompted us to suddenly see the car and run in opposite directions? I believe an angel sent by God pushed Stacey sideways. I believe Bryna never hit the cement, but landed on an angel's hand. I have no other explanation. Hebrews 1:14 tells us that angels are ministering spirits sent to serve us. Sometimes we can see them and sometimes they are invisible. Hebrews 13:2 reminds us to entertain strangers, for by doing so, we might actually be entertaining angels without knowing it. Artists depict them with wings, but when we see them, they can be mistaken for real people. There is an unseen world out there that is just as real as the seen world.

In his book *Angels*, Billy Graham tells the story of John Patton and his wife, who were missionaries in the Hebrides Islands. Language barriers caused the natives to become hostile. On one terror-filled night, they surrounded the Pattons' hut with flaming torches as they moved in to set their house on fire and then kill them. And then, for some unexplainable reason, the natives suddenly turned and ran off into the woods.

A year later, when the chief of the tribe became a Christian, John Patton asked him about the aborted attack. "Tell me what happened. It looked like you were going to burn us out and kill us. And then you all turned and ran away. What happened?"

The chief responded, "All those soldiers you had in shining armor had their spears drawn. We were afraid."

The chief reported seeing hundreds of big men in shining garments circling the mission station. Though the soldiers were not visible to the Pattons, the tribesmen fortunately saw them.

I wish I could take a one-day vacation to heaven. Surely God must have a secretary somewhere in the heavenlies. I want to ask questions about the near fatality on the road, the almost cracked head on the door jamb, and whatever happened at the slide. What is the rest of the story? I have more stories like these with the same questions.

The only problem is that I have not heard of round-trip tickets to heaven. My other plan is to write out my list and have someone slip it in my hand when I die, so that it will go with me. I fear that when I get to heaven I will be so caught up with my new life I will forget my questions. The problem with this plan is that material things like lists don't seem to accompany those that have passed on. So, my list continues to get longer and my excitement over hearing the rest of the story intensifies.

Consider the following:

My first car cost only $500. It was a flashy red car with sporty hubcaps. Not being exactly brand-new, the car had some mechanical mishaps. Before venturing on my thirty-five-mile commute between my home and college, I always took time to pray. The car and I had some unusual adventures, but our mechanical mishaps were rather inexpensive. One time a radiator hose burst on the freeway, and a man from a house hidden over a hill came to my rescue with water. Another time a fan belt broke, and a man pulled over to help me. He had a fan belt in his car, which he installed in my car. Seriously! He told me he travelled back and forth just looking for people to help. Really?

One cold, foggy morning, in another car, I was on the way to school with all four children when I ran out of gas. That time a gentleman pushed me with his car to a gas station. When I got out of my car to thank him, he was gone. Totally gone! Who was he? How could he disappear so fast?

A favorite story is the time I had a flat tire on my way to a Bible study. I pulled off the road and decided to do my best in jacking up the car. My first error was putting the jack in the wheel well. That is not where you jack up a car. A man in an expensive suit stopped to help me by kindly relocating my jack to the bumper of the car. Another man dressed up in mechanic clothes stopped by and told the businessman he would take over, since his clothes were better fitted for the job. When the mechanic learned I was on my way to a Bible study, he launched into his own sermon on the importance of finding the right church for one's family. Who talks about that topic to a complete stranger? He had no way of knowing the church I had grown up in had split, the pastor had considered suicide, and I was wrestling with following my husband into a church we both loved or remaining loyal to a remnant congregation in the church my extended family was still attending. Dave and I had visited a church that had seemed so wonderful for our children and for us. But I felt we needed to be loyal to our frail church and to the pastor, who was truly suffering. The tire-changing mechanic kept emphasizing how important it was to find a church that was right for one's entire family. He didn't change topics, but added personal illustrations without any encouraging comments from me. It was a monologue, and I was the audience. Thankfully, his sermon freed me to follow the desires of my heart and the leadership of my husband. I never told him my dilemma. The next Sunday I followed his advice and our family gained so much from the new church. I don't know who that man was, but his sermon was sent to us from God.

Isn't it great that we are not left alone to figure out everything for ourselves? God intervenes in our lives. We see His interventions through our friends and circumstances. And we see shadows of interventions from the unseen world. I don't know how many angels may have been sent my way, but I expect there is a heavenly host much larger than I imagine. My list of questions is growing, and I look forward to hearing the rest of the story! I hope I will never forget the questions on my list.

Chapter 9

SHADOWS

I WOULD LIKE to say that life is full of roses and sunshine and God sends angels to always rescue us from any tribulation. And Dave and Marlys lived happily ever after with their four beautiful daughters. The end.

Life is not a fairy tale. God is not Santa Claus. Good and evil coexist. Every person experiences pain.

Where is God during the good times and the bad? Where, you say? We both know He is right there beside us; right there hugging us; right there carrying us through the times; right there weeping with us. He is the Almighty God who is not so high and mighty that He lives abstractly away from our real lives. No, He is here with us, as if we were the only person in His world. He cares about us and loves us a thousand times more than we love ourselves.

Bryna Lynn, born May 16th, 1980, was the youngest of our four daughters. As she lay there beside me in bed, I wondered what personality would emerge from this little one. What talents lay hidden inside her? What would be the bents in her personality that I needed to respect in my parenting? I didn't want to train her to be a math teacher if God gifted her for being a nurse. I prayed, "Lord, help me to follow Your leading in raising this beautiful baby girl. I give her to You, and I thank You for the privilege of being her mom. If You intend to raise her up as a missionary, I give her to You." Little did I know how that prayer would be answered. Bryna did become a missionary, but not in the sense of foreign missions which I had pictured. Instead, she was a missionary to me. She changed my beliefs and challenged my walk. How I miss her.

One nurse shocked me by saying, "Your baby has a temper like no other."

Another nurse stated, "Little Bryna is really strong. Lying on her tummy, she rose up in her bassinet and looked around the nursery." She was probably scoping out her game plan, for she always seemed to be one step ahead of me. Where was the "You have the sweetest baby ever!"?

The "sweet baby" comment did eventually come. Her elementary school teacher confided, "If I had to give an award for the sweetest child in this school, it would go to Bryna."

Physically strong, Bryna was the only first grader in her school who could scamper up the giant rope hanging from the gymnasium ceiling. As an infant, she could work her way out of the infant car seats, even when we wrapped ropes around the sections of the car seat to hold it together. She hated wearing her shoes in the car. Tied in double knots, they still came off and hid themselves in secret places in the car. Her middle name should have been Houdini! Before she learned to walk, she crawled at lightning speed to the forbidden road in front of our house. One person leaving a door or gate slightly ajar, and she was gone.

Wanting to be the perfect mother, I made all her baby food. No food colorings or preservatives for my child! But, when I ran out of prepared food, I tried to sneak in a jar of the toddler baby food. Bryna, only a few months old, somehow clued in, and refused to eat it. I tried everything! I tried adding extra seasonings, warming it up without her seeing me take it from the jar, sprinkling shredded cheese on top … every time I tried using a purchased, convenient dinner from baby food jars, she refused to eat.

When Bryna was nine months old, she contracted a violent case of herpes mouth sores, which filled her mouth with hundreds of sores and even caused her face to swell up with puffy cheeks. She refused to drink or eat. After wrestling with her for twenty minutes, I finally managed to pry her mouth open and force her to take a narcotic pain reliever ordered by the doctor so she could sleep. The long three- or four-hour sleep predicted by the doctor lasted only forty-five minutes, which was hardly worth the effort of fighting her over administering the narcotic drug. Our only choice left was hospitalization. Grim. One month earlier, Bryna had been hospitalized for pneumonia. She did not win popularity points when she kept tearing down the plastic breathing tents. Shoes were made to come off, car seats were made to come apart, and breathing tents were for crashing down. Not relishing the idea of another hospital visit, I tried trickery.

Plan A: "Bryna, let's have a tea party!" She was pleasantly amused as I set out tiny cups and little plates and stirred up a delicious milkshake. What fun. We sat down in our little chairs while I poured the milkshake into each of our cups. "Let's drink our milkshake." No way. Her mouth was clamped shut as she turned her face away from me.

Let's try involving God.

Plan B: "Bryna, we are going on a walk and we are going to praise God, because He is going to do a miracle." She looked up at me with serious eyes as if to say, "My mom has totally flipped out." I bundled her up in a warm coat and hat for this cold February day, and we headed out for a neighborhood stroller walk. We did not just pray praises to God. No we did not. We sang them. We sang loudly. I walked into a neighbor's yard and bent a flower down to Bryna's face so she could smell the sweet fragrance. "This is the flower that God made. Thank you, God, for Your beautiful flowers. And look, there is a bird pecking for seeds. Thank you, God, for the birds." We trespassed yards in delight over God's creation. We petted dogs in the name of Jesus. We sang. We prayed. We praised God. Yes we did. And then we returned home to our tea party table. "Look, Bryna, our tea party. Thank you, God, for this lovely tea party." I handed her the cup of milkshake, and gulp, gulp, gulp. She gulped it down and cried for more. "Thank you, thank you, thank you, God." We did not go to the hospital and she recovered.

Summers in Texas are designed for swimming pools. Scurrying through household chores in the mornings, we joined friends for afternoon swims at the public pool. Bryna was four years old and soon became bored with jumping off the side of the pool. Even though she did not know how to swim, she wanted to jump off the diving board. "Bryna, you can't jump off the diving board, because you don't know how to swim." Reasoning bypassed her brain processes. She still begged to jump off the diving board. Distracting her with silly games didn't work. Her mind was set on the diving pool. "OK. We will go to the lifeguard and ask him if you can jump off the diving board. If he says 'no,' then we will stay in the swimming pool." She agreed.

"My daughter wants to jump off the low diving board. Is it OK for her to do that?"

"Sure."

"But, she can't swim."

"You can get in the water to catch her."

Oh my goodness, this was not a good plan. Bryna ran over to the board as I jumped in to "catch" her. With a big smile on her face, she launched herself into the air. There was no catch. An explosion of water followed her entry into the abyss. Down she sank as I frantically tried to see her through all the water. I could only see bubbles and darkness below me. It seemed forever before she jubilantly surfaced with laughter. "I want to do that again." I spent the summer watching her jump and assisting her to the edge where she could "do it again."

Environmental stimulations sometimes overwhelmed Bryna. I was unaware of this problem until we attempted school shopping for her kindergarten year. Having spent nearly an hour trying on clothes and selecting outfits, I was excited with her choices. Suddenly she stiffened, her eyes darting around the store.

"We have to leave. I want to get out of here."

"But Bryna, we have not purchased the clothes."

"I don't want them. I want to get out of here."

She was frantic. I somehow managed to hurriedly get to the counter, pay, and leave.

Through the years, Bryna learned some coping skills. Shopping with her turned into an interesting experience. She developed a hilarious "walk-by" style in her adult life that I truly miss sharing with her now. She would drive us to the Target store, and we walked at a fast clip down the aisles. If a cute blouse caught her attention, we stopped, spent about ten seconds admiring it, and moved on at our quick pace. We might take a detour to revisit something seen on a previous trip, or we might continue directly to whatever we came to purchase. I might see something that interested me and we took a few moments to look at it together. But after a few minutes in the store, she would have the "gotta leave now" feeling and out we went.

Sometimes we left with purchases; other times we had nothing. Once out of the store, she processed the walk-by examinations to determine if another walk-by was needed for purchase considerations. Later in the week, she might make three or more walk-by trips to the store before actually purchasing an item. Impulse shopping was not her weakness!

Shadows of difficulties ahead began to emerge. From all her memorization of phonics in kindergarten, I had high hopes for her first-grade year. Listening to her read books she brought home, I asked the teacher if she might qualify for the challenge classes. Quite the opposite happened! It turned out that she was memorizing books so that when two pages stuck together, I heard her read the precise words on the wrong page. Her teacher placed her in a pull-out program where she received additional help from a teacher she adored.

Tragedy struck in third grade when she was raped by her friend's seventh-grade brother. Adding to this horror, Bryna kept the event secret. Three years later she was plagued by voices which told her not to look in the window, or she would die. The voices told her there was an odd number of students in the class, and if she were eliminated, everything would work so much better for students to pair up with each other.

Even though her reading improved, Bryna could not pass spelling tests. We worked hours together on a single spelling list. We split words into symbols, invented games, tried visual learning skills. We would be encouraged the night before the test when it seemed she had the words mastered. And then she came home with 20 percent correct. It was devastating. I told her that the spelling part of her brain was not working right now, but it would eventually. I reminded her continually that she was intelligent, and we took breaks from our spelling work. And then, a couple weeks later, we worked again. She asked me frequently, "Why is school so hard for me?"

My heart breaks for those millions of children who may not be gifted in the verbal or math skills, but who have intelligences that our school system is unable to appreciate: artistic intelligence, music intelligence, kinesthetic intelligence, and social interaction intelligence. Spelling and reading are easy for me; not so for the Brynas of this world. But I admire Bryna's insight into personalities, her wit, her humor, her servant's heart, her love for those our society walks by without noticing. She was blind to the beautiful parts of her personality and aware only of her weaknesses. My heart cries out for the Brynas of this world.

In her sixth-grade year, after I left for school in the morning, Bryna drank Clorox to end her life. Teryl, two years older, came to her rescue. I can hardly write about this day; it hurts so much. Several close friends, my family, doctors, questions, confusion … The hospital recommended we place her in a psychiatric hospital, one that was supposed to be the best on the West Coast. Numb, shaken, frightened, we followed their advice. If I could relive making that decision, I would fight to take her home. We thought we were making a decision in her best interest.

Little did I know we were embarking on a journey that would consume fifteen years. Bryna, our missionary, had so much to teach us. We thank God for her life and her love. When I look into the brown eyes of her beloved dog, Zoey, I remember how she kept saying, "How can you say no to such a cute face?"

How can we say "yes" to the Brynas of this world? How can we say, "Yes, you are precious in the sight of God"? "Yes, you are His unique creation." "Yes, the world is a better place because of you." "Yes, we love you."

I don't know who is reading this. But if you are struggling in areas of your life and beating yourself up because you don't measure up to your own expectations, remember Bryna. People love you deeply, as people loved Bryna. People see you differently than you see yourself. And most importantly, you were created by God, who never makes junk. He has beautiful designs for your life. It doesn't matter what inadequacies you feel or traumas you have experienced. God knows your heart and He understands you better than you understand yourself, for He created you. Look to Him. Ask Him to help you receive His love. He hears your prayers and He always answers.

Chapter 10

VALLEY

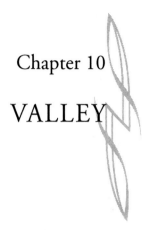

BRYNA'S HOSPITALIZATION AND the years thereafter form a dark chapter for my family. I thought of journaling during it, but the pain was too great to repeat again on paper.

Have you noticed how pain seems to come in layers? As we gathered together in the emergency room, our hearts plummeted when the doctor strongly advised Bryna's placement in a psychiatric hospital. She was considered to be at high risk for another suicide attempt. Adding to the turmoil, Bryna was adamantly opposed to the plan. And yet, the doctor assured us that the hospital he had chosen was the "best on the West Coast." The thought of placing Bryna against her wishes was extremely painful.

Adding to that layer of pain was the pain of feeling like failures as parents. Where did we go wrong? Another huge layer of pain was the abandonment our other three children would feel as we poured out for Bryna. I have to add that all three girls loved their sister. They gave their all for Bryna sacrificially. And then, of course, another layer of pain was the abandonment Bryna would experience as she was torn from our family and placed in a hospital. There were a multitude of layers, for no one suffers alone.

No beds were vacant in the preteen section where Bryna should have been placed. So she was admitted into the teen section. We thought she would be admitted for only two or three days. I will never forget the pain of walking away from her on the day of admission. Never. And then later I saw the dried food hanging from the ceiling from long-ago food fights; I heard the screams of children fighting back; I learned of the three-point restraints and then the five-point restraints. Questioning why some children were in hospital gowns, I learned that clothes were taken away as a form of punishment. The language was street language filled with cursing. Bryna, who never wanted to stay overnight at any friend's home, was now forced to live in an environment so different from her own home.

The three days ventured into five days, a week, two weeks … Bryna begged to come home. I encountered her pleas with what I thought was tough love. It was so hard. Telephone calls were gut-wrenching. My trust was in her counselors and case manager, who assured me she was being given great care. I had no trust in my parenting skills. I felt like a total failure. Dave visited her every day, a three-hour commute after work. I visited every other day, because I also wanted to be with our children at home. I was teaching full time, trying to be a mother to my three daughters, and spending time with Bryna.

Lynell, Stacey, and Teryl made many visits with us. We brought games to play with Bryna and joined her in counseling sessions.

The days were a blur. I cried and prayed. On the way to work, I crossed over the Narrows Bridge which joined the cities of Gig Harbor and Tacoma. On one side of the bridge I mentally dumped my home problems and picked up my math teacher bundle as I drove to work. On the way home, I picked up the home burden again. It was a heavy load.

A psychiatrist at the hospital encouraged us to seek a psychological evaluation for Bryna, which might unlock some doors, since Bryna refused to talk through any of her feelings. Insurance would not cover the $1,200, and in those days, that was a large amount of money for us. We took the financial plunge, hoping root problems would surface. Bryna, Dave, and I, along with Teryl and Stacey, were summoned into a conference room. I wanted to take notes, but was told none of us were allowed to take notes. I did not have to take notes, because his words have been indelibly written on my brain. The psychiatrist said he had three things to share. I was excited. We had sacrificed financially to hear these words, and now we would know what we could do to turn Bryna's life around. This psychiatrist would unlock the prison doors and set Bryna free.

"First of all, Bryna has below-average intelligence."

What? Did he really say that? With Bryna right here beside us? A dagger flew into my heart. He just undid all those hundreds of evenings when Bryna and I worked through spelling words and my telling her she was bright and intelligent. The spelling gene didn't pass on to Bryna, but intelligence isn't just about reading and writing. She was intelligent, and now this man tore down in one sentence the hundreds of hours of building up Bryna. Volcanic storms swooshed in my stomach. I didn't say anything, hoping Bryna had not heard what he said. I just have to add here, in this writing, that he was dead wrong. Yes, Bryna was closed up and speaking in fragmented sentence structures, but she grew up into a lovely young lady who was extremely articulate, witty, and rich in humor. She demonstrated wisdom and discernment beyond her years. That man was dead wrong.

"Secondly, I believe Dave ·..."

He accused Dave of something that was totally, and thankfully, not true. I was about to ask questions in Dave's defense when the third dagger launched into the air.

"Last of all, I showed pictures to Bryna and let her describe what she saw. There was one showing two people running. Bryna described the picture as her mom and her racing. I believe Bryna feels in competition with her mother."

That third dagger hit the core of my mother's heart. I felt personally speared, like never before. The volcano inside me erupted and I leapt up from the table, ending the shortest ever conference with a psychiatrist. I took off running at full speed.

I had spent long evenings with Bryna, helping her with schoolwork and encouraging her in every way I could. I desperately wanted her to feel better about herself. And now she was saying that I was in competition with her; that somehow I was making life harder for her, not easier. I ran fast and hard to wherever. I wanted to get totally lost, to never be found. I weaved in and out of housing developments, hoping to lose sight of true north. What kind of a mother is in competition with her daughter? A bad mother. I cried and prayed, "God, I am totally unfit to be a mother. I have failed with a capital F." For twenty minutes I ran aimlessly, totally broken. I decided it was wrong for me to be her mother. "So, God, she needs to go into a group home. I am not fit to be her mother. I have done a miserable job. I have poured out in every way I know, and it is all summed up with my being in competition with her." A few running steps later, "But God, not just any group home. I want her in a good group home." Why do I care if the home is a good home? Is it because I do love her? What is my definition of "good home"? God broke through my confusion. "Yes, I do care about her. Yes, I do love her. And yes, I do still want to be her mother." I looked around me and somehow had not managed to get lost. I turned back toward the hospital. I loved her and I cared about her and I still wanted to be her mother. Dave and Stacey and Teryl had spread out looking for me. I spotted Stacey a block away and ran into her outstretched arms. We were all scared and confused.

Three days later, Bryna called from the hospital.

"Ya know what the doctor said about the picture?"

"Yes, Bryna."

"Well, I didn't mean like we were racing. I meant like we were running on the beach."

"You mean, like we were running for fun?"

"Yes. We were just running together on the beach."

"Oh, Bryna, you don't know how much this call means to me. I love you so very, very much. Thank you, thank you for telling me this. It means everything to me."

I thank God that He did not leave me for weeks or months or years with the lie of being in competition with Bryna tormenting my spirit. I am so thankful that Bryna reached out to me with truth. I believed her.

Lies keep us locked inside prison doors. I am so thankful to God, so thankful that He revealed the truth so quickly for me. He didn't leave me imprisoned with that horrible lie, but

He unlocked that prison door and released me into freedom. Lies imprison us; truth makes prisoners free. Glory hallelujah!

I should have purchased stock in the Kleenex company, for I am quite a case right now … praising God and crying and pacing the floor as I attempt to get this written. How many children, how many parents, are suffering intensely with lies they believe are true? Do you feel imprisoned? Worthless? Condemned? Ugly? What is the lie keeping your prison door shut? Break down that door in the name of Jesus. Kick the door with gusto! Say "no" to Satan, the author of lies, and say "yes" to God. You can't listen to both at the same time. Choose to whom you will listen. Choose wisely. This choice will make all the difference in your life.

I pray in the name of Jesus that any lie holding you captive will be revealed to you. I pray that the quiet voice of the Holy Spirit will speak truth to you and that you will claim it as your truth. May you feel the love of God poured down on you mightily as you walk through that prison door, never to return to the dark and cold dungeon. God loves you a thousand times more than you love yourself. Believe that truth. If you can't believe it, then pray God will help you believe it. Pray for it a hundred times in a day until you believe. Tell God you are having trouble believing and keep repeating the truth and praying you can believe. Do whatever it takes to break down the strongholds of lies in your life that are destroying you. The truth is that God created you and loves you more than you have ever loved anyone, because He is infinite in His love. We are only finite creatures. Have you forgiven people for some bad things that happened to you? I am sure you have. Your forgiveness toward others is only finite. God's forgiveness is infinite. He forgives you for anything that is keeping your prison door locked. Look to Him; believe what He says to you. There is no sin too big for God to forgive. Behold, the Lamb of God takes away the sins of the world and makes captives free. Walk forward in the freedom of truth.

One day I drove to the supermarket for food. I remember going down all the aisles with my cart, finding nothing, and leaving the store with nothing. I couldn't find anything to eat in a grocery store! I stood in my kitchen and turned around in circles. My brain was in overload, I didn't know what to cook for dinner, and my heart was dying.

Thankfully, I had the sense to call someone in our church and ask for help with meals. I am so grateful for those meals people brought to us once or twice a week for a couple months. Sometimes we need to ask for help. Don't be afraid to ask for help. People need people.

In the dark valleys, God's light and love still penetrate the darkness. Prior to going into the hospital, Bryna had wanted a bunny. Having been through the hamster fiasco, I was not encouraging in regards to adding a rabbit. But with Bryna's despair, I grabbed at any opportunity to spur her on to healing. "When you leave this hospital, we will find you a baby bunny. You just need to get well." Maybe a bunny would provide the motivation she needed for getting well.

"A chocolate-colored bunny?"

"Yes, a chocolate-colored bunny!"

Three months of hospitalization behind us, Bryna and I drove to a pet store with three chocolate-colored bunnies for sale. As Bryna attempted to cuddle the first bunny, it jumped out of her hands and scampered into the cage. The second bunny reacted just like the first one. But the third bunny snuggled into her shoulder. Fudge, a chocolate-colored dwarf bunny, was the keeper!

What fun to watch little Fudge, who could snuggle in Bryna's cupped hands, suddenly jump two feet into the air as she hopped throughout our house. School was out for the summer and Bryna and Fudge spent two glorious weeks together.

Darkness struck again with a psychiatric relapse. A fire raging inside of Bryna exploded into an unsafe temper toward Teryl and a butcher knife in Bryna's drawer. No one was hurt, but we were torn into shreds emotionally. Our home suddenly was not a safe place for Teryl or Bryna. Tearing Bryna away from Fudge was not fun.

A couple weeks into her second hospitalization, I realized that Fudge was growing fast from bunny into rabbit. If she became full grown before Bryna returned home, she would no longer seem like Bryna's rabbit. I decided that Bryna needed to see this bunny grow up. Bryna needed to be a part of the process. Bryna had to see Fudge. I determined she would see Fudge.

Fudge, being a little bit bigger than a grapefruit, fit perfectly inside my handbag. Yes she did! The purse had a little flap that snapped shut, and I inserted Fudge and slung my purse over my shoulder. Inspectors always looked for metal items we might be carrying, but never for bunnies! Dave and I slipped through the inspection, met up with Bryna, lowered the purse under the table, and told Bryna to lift up the flap. She was astonished that I would do such a thing!

"Mom, I can't believe you did this!" We played for an hour with little Fudge. I finally reinserted the bunny, and off we went.

A couple days later, without the bunny, I met up with personnel in the hallway.

"I did something on my last visit here which MAY (notice my choice of words—pretending to be oh, so innocent) have broken hospital policy."

"You mean when you brought the rabbit?"

Oh my goodness! They knew what we had done. I gulped a weak "Yes. That was what I was referring to."

"Well, the doctor has decided to use the bunny as positive reinforcement. We would like to have you bring the rabbit in when Bryna makes steps of progress. Will that work for you?"

"Oh yes, that works perfectly!"

I was so excited! It wasn't long before I was told that Fudge needed to come. This time I came waltzing into the hospital with Fudge in my arms.

"Oh no, you can't come in here with a rabbit," warned the receptionist.

Trying not to be sassy and proud, I managed to be as polite as possible: "It is doctor's orders." I wanted to sing "NAna NAna NAAna." All my insides were jumping up and down and shouting, "This is more fun than Disneyland. The rules are falling apart and Fudge wins!"

"Which doctor?" People scrambled, and to their consternation, found the orders. Never had such orders been written. What were they to do? They finally asked a head administrator to escort us down the hall into a fenced-in area of grass just outside Bryna's unit. He had to lean against the building a full half hour, watching us while Bryna and Fudge gallantly played. I have to confess an inner satisfaction leaping up within me just to see an administrator pulled away from all their important duties to watch a hurting child play with a bunny.

Fudge was a bright spot in the dark valley. This second hospitalization took some bad turns. Dave kept coming home with the next bad report. Bryna's condition worsened. Our sweet, timid daughter was no longer an alien in the teen culture. She assumed their language, lost her clothes due to rebellion, and was put into the five-point restraints. Medication was increased until she became ramrod stiff, turned pale, and looked like she was dying. Dave kept coming home with one more bad report. One night, as we were going to bed, he told me the last bad turn of events.

I got up and fell on my knees in the living room, crying in desperation and hopelessness.

Bryna was getting worse. We were losing her, and I had no answers. Weeping, I lifted my arms upward and cried out to God. Words of Psalm 23 came to my mind.

"The Lord is my shepherd."

"Lord, You are Bryna's shepherd. Do you see her? She is bleeding and broken. She is Your special sheep. She hurts like no other. Where are You? Where? I see. Yes, I see her head rests on Your shoulder. Yes, You are holding her in Your arms. You are her loving Heavenly Father. You are with her. Thank you, Jesus." I am abbreviating the conversation, but you understand how it flowed.

"The Lord is my shepherd, I shall not want."

"Do you see her needs? Oh my goodness! She has big needs. Lord, look at her. Do you see the needs? She starves to feel loved. She feels like a misfit in Your flock, misunderstood, broken. She wants to run in freedom, but sticker bushes grab at her fur and entangle her in briars. What are You saying? You are the Good Shepherd. You see all Your sheep and You are caring for them. I can trust You with Bryna. You love her with Your infinite love. Thank you, Jesus."

I prayed through the twenty-third Psalm phrase by phrase until I came to the part:

"Yea, though I walk through the valley of the shadow of death, I will…" I couldn't even say the next word. The scriptural text is: "Yea, though I walk through the valley of the shadow of death, I will *fear* no evil." I could not say the word "fear." I cried bitterly and knew then, when I could not even say the word "fear," that my fears consumed me. My fears were the overwhelming emotion that coursed through me. I poured them out one by one. "What if she loses her mental capabilities permanently? What if she becomes mentally ill for the rest of her life? What if she dies in the hospital?" I laid them at the feet of Jesus. I lifted her up into the arms of Jesus. I knew she belonged more to God than to me. He knew what was best for Bryna. Her suffering was intense and I could trust that He would care for her. I lifted her up like I had lifted Stacey up several years earlier. "If she becomes mentally handicapped, we will love on her. If she becomes mentally ill, we will seek Your guidance and we will embrace her life. Lord, if You have to take her, it will be well with our souls. I want the best for Bryna. I know her suffering has been painful." Although I truly wanted her to come through this, I also wanted God's perfect plan for Bryna. God met me in that moment. I can't explain it, but I know it happened. An unexpected, supernatural peace flowed into my whole being a second time in my life. My tears were wiped away and I knew Bryna was under the care of Jesus. This whole encounter lasted about twenty minutes and I was back in bed for a sound sleep. Unbelievable, but true!

Days later, staff informed us that Bryna had experienced a psychotic episode, which might be the beginning of a series of them. I would normally have been disturbed by such a report, but the peace given to me still consumed me in a way that I can't quite explain, except that it was a gift of God's presence. As things turned out, the psychotic instances occurred a couple times at home, once Bryna was discharged, and then never returned. Thank you, Jesus.

As I expressed earlier, God's light and love still penetrated the dark times. It took many years for the light of truth to shine. Bryna believed the lie that her family hospitalized her so we could "get rid of her." Somehow she imagined us all laughing and dancing while she was imprisoned in darkness. In truth, the exact opposite occurred. I often wish the many counselors who talked with Bryna in her middle school and high school years had talked with her parents also so that they could have dispelled some of the lies, which became life threatening. I don't know what was said behind all the closed doors. But I do know that closed doors shut out truth. When does confidentiality in counseling foster lies and become life threatening? If the counseling doors had swung open to include Bryna's parents, would she be alive today? I have questions, no great answers.

The truth of not being able to see backward as we move forward stills the voices of self-condemnation. There are many parents out there like me, trying to do their best in directing their children. Looking backwards, I wish we had not hospitalized her. The hospital we chose has been a great place for many people we have known. But for Bryna, even though some good things came out of it, there were a myriad of bad results. What should we have done? I am not sure. She was considered high risk for repeated suicidal episodes. I wish I had not been so quick to condemn myself and had more confidence in my own parenting. I am not sure how things would have changed. But the truth is, we can only live in the forward direction. I have to forgive myself, knowing I acted out of a heart of purity toward Bryna. I desperately tried doing the right thing, but I am an imperfect person with a short vision of the future.

The truth is none of us is a perfect parent. This is not an excuse to act carelessly, but it is a good reminder when the lies of rotten parenting accusations attack. The truth that parents can't protect their children from every bad thing will dispel the lies of self-condemnation. Sin is in the world, and bad things happen to good people, to the innocent, to everyone.

So where is God when bad things happen? Right beside us. As you continue seeing this story unfold through the next chapters, you will see God's presence.

Before closing this chapter, I want to share one more instance of God's love shining in our dark valley. Cookies 'n' Cream, nicknamed Cookies, was our border collie, full of life and vitality. Living on thirty acres of woods, Cookies delighted in greeting us with front porch delectables such as dead rats, dead squirrels, dead snakes. You get the picture. Returning home from one of our visits with Bryna during her second hospitalization, we found Cookies walking toward our porch with a dead bunny draped over his mouth; a chocolate-colored bunny, just like Fudge. It was Fudge! We don't know how Fudge escaped the confines of our house, but here she was in Cookies' mouth, dead. How were we ever going to explain this to Bryna? I grabbed the saliva-coated bunny from Cookies and felt a rapid heartbeat. She was not dead? How could this be? What do I do with a traumatized bunny? What did I do for traumatized babies? Sing "Jesus Loves Me"! I gently lifted little Fudge up to my shoulder and spoke calmly and slowly as we found our way to the couch.

"Precious little Fudge, beloved bunny, God loves you. Jesus loves you. He cares about your mishaps. Oh little Fudge, we pray for you. We pray God will heal you in Jesus' name. We pray all your internal organs will be healed. We pray God's peace upon you. In the name of Jesus, we pray for a miracle." And then I began softly singing,

"Jesus loves me this I know,
for the Bible tells me so.
Little ones to Him belong;
They are weak, but HE IS STRONG!
Yes, Jesus loves Fudge.
Yes, Jesus loves Fudge.
Yes, Jesus loves Fudge.
The Bible tells us so."

As I sang over Fudge, her heart rate slowed way down to normal bunny heart rate. And then I questioned my parenting skills once again. Did bunnies like to be cuddled up to our shoulders? Did they really like to be held? I lowered her to my lap and quit holding her so she could have freedom to do whatever she wanted to do. She tried scurrying up to my shoulder. Yes, bunnies like to be held. We sat a long time singing and praying together. When I tried giving her water through her water spigot, her mouth was bleeding and so badly swollen that she could not grip onto the spigot. I had no idea what internal injuries she must be suffering from, and prayed she would make it through the night. And she did. Royally! By morning she was eating solid food.

When I shared our miracle bunny story with the doctor, he said we did not understand how big the miracle really was. When captured by animals, rabbits will typically die of heart attacks from the trauma of being captured before they are actually chewed upon. God must have wanted to wave a flag in front of us to tell us He was with us, through everything, dark as it was. Thank you, Jesus. When I get to heaven, I want to hear the whole story! I want to know, God, did You send angels to clear the traffic so we could drive home just at the right instant? Did You assign an angel to keep Cookies' mouth open and unable to clamp down on Fudge? What were You doing behind the scenes? I want to hear the rest of the story! Remind me, God, when I get to heaven to ask for the rest of the story.

Dearly beloved Fudge far outlived the typical dwarf bunny. She was nearly ten years old when she died. God's ways are mysterious and we cannot fathom them. Thank you, God, for loving us and caring about the details of our lives.

Chapter 11

TOUGH LOVE VS. GRACE

WAR AND PEACE, love and hate, justice and mercy … life is full of opposites. When do we stand up for the oppressed and bring war to the oppressors? When do we stand for peace when there is dissension? What things demand our love? What things demand our hate? When do we show justice and punishment, and when do we extend mercy? It is easy to ask the questions, difficult to give the answers.

Relationships between people are full of questions and contradictions. I think one of the toughest tensions in parenting is knowing when to administer tough love and when to extend grace.

It helps to have the big picture in mind. My consuming goal for my children was to know God and to love God. The other goals of academic growth, athletic development, behavior modification, etc. were subsidiary to the big goal of falling in love with Jesus. I knew that if they followed Jesus out of love, He would direct their paths. Likewise, if I learned to love Jesus with all my heart, He would direct me in the parenting paths I should take. Unfortunately, we all stumble along those paths and stray onto wrong trails. But God keeps calling us back to the right trail.

It is so easy for us as parents to get caught up with the small pictures and forget the big pictures. We end up driving our kids to frustration and rebellion with all our rules and opinions, which are focused on the small picture rather than the big picture. We take a "would-be librarian" and try to mold him into a football player. We complain about the little things our children do wrong and forget to praise them for the big things they do right. We honor our A-student child and ask why our C-student child can't be more like his sister.

In the early years of elementary school, one of my daughters adopted the new fashion statement of wearing her hair in a funny ponytail that hung from the side of her head like a tassel on a graduation cap. Even though I did not like the style, I kept my mouth shut, which I am not always so good at doing. She asked me before taking off to school, "How does my hair look?"

I answered honestly, "I love the shine in your hair. Your hair has a beautiful bounce to it!" I knew eventually the silly pony-tail would go. It took about five months of waiting, but the tail did leave.

In the high school years, another one of my daughters had her bedroom floor so cluttered with papers and stuff that one would walk throughout the room several inches above floor level. Not exaggerating! I was after her to clean up her room. And she was always so ready to do it in another couple days, which never seemed to come. Sometimes we tackled it together, but most of the time I posed threats. When she did get it cleaned up, it was only a matter of a short time before it was once again in the impossible state of disorder. This war between us was dividing us. She was doing excellent work at school, was active in her youth group, and ran with endurance on her cross-country team. She was honoring God in her life, and the bedroom floor was just not on the top of her priority list. I decided to withdraw from the battle, focus on the big picture of my daughter loving God and following His leading for her, and forget the small picture of the perfect house. When she moved out to be married, we found dirty plates under the bed. However, the amazing part is that the floor was so covered with heaps of paper and stuff that the carpet underneath was carefully protected from any stains. It looked brand-new. And to her credit today, housekeeping has moved its way up her priority list. She now loves God with all her heart and has a clean house, all at the same time. Amazing! I backed out of the way, and God showed up in her life. Love it!

There is a tricky balance between giving instructions, demanding certain performances, and letting go of our desires so God can grab their hearts. There are no formulas and no clear answers, just the quiet leading of the Holy Spirit who speaks to us.

When Bryna was finally discharged from the hospital the second and last time, we were hit with the tension of tough love versus grace. It was a hard journey for us, and we erred on both sides of the perfect balance point, with our error score exceeding our right-moves score.

Whereas Bryna was filled with tears of gratitude over being back in church after her first three-month stint in the hospital, she was now adamantly opposed to going to church. Whereas curse words were not heard in our home, now her sentences were filled with them. She crawled on all fours to get past windows, for she feared voices would tell her they were out to kill her. She hated Jesus, because He was way too perfect, and she was angry with us. Hard times.

What was the big picture? She was not the Bryna we once knew. Her body looked the same, but everything else seemed different. We oscillated between closing our ears to the abrasive words, thankful that she was at last verbalizing, and demanding baby-step changes in behavior. Our top priority was the physical safety of Teryl. Bryna had raging anger within her that she did not know how to handle. Her issues of being victimized sexually on top of feeling abandonment from her own family merged with her own insecurities and academic weaknesses, condemning her as unfit to even exist.

There are people reading this who can identify with Bryna, and others who can identify with her parents or sisters. Tough stuff.

The road of healing was not easy. It had many bumps, and all our children suffered in varying degrees. Dave and I were in a quandary as to what we needed to do. We sought the help of experts and prayed for God's wisdom. We tried instant cures that never worked. We wanted to fix Bryna when God wanted to change us.

My dream of Bryna being a missionary was fulfilled. I was thinking foreign missions, God was thinking home missions. She changed us all. We learned lessons in giving unconditional love. Our three daughters gave sacrificially to Bryna. Lynell turned down a summer job opportunity near her California college to spend the summer with Bryna at our home. She found a job close to our home. Stacey poured out hours of time talking with Bryna, reasoning with her, trying to help her through the processing. Teryl, only two years older than Bryna, remained loyal and faithful to Bryna while Bryna lashed out at her verbally. Jealous of Teryl's success socially and academically, and frustrated with her own struggles, Bryna's hurts ran deep. And hurting people hurt others. We all hurt, and we all hurt each other. But I also saw forgiveness of my children toward one another.

Bryna also modeled sacrificial love. I planned to hurry home from work, throw together a chicken enchilada recipe, and take it to a faculty party. When I arrived home, Bryna was putting it into the oven. She had totally prepared the entire recipe. What a lift to my spirits! This was not a one-time occurrence, for she was always looking for ways to lessen my load.

Bryna continued to receive counseling and we continued being on the outside of those closed doors. The counselors were a thread of hope for Bryna while the confidentiality created walls of lies.

The main theme during these black years was the theme of unconditional love, exhibited by all of Bryna's sisters and by Dave and me. Eventually our love, the love of other significant people who poured tons of time into Bryna's life, and the love of Jesus penetrated Bryna's heart, and things slowly changed in a positive direction.

God loves us unconditionally and gives us abundant mercy. We come to Him easily, because He treats us gently. As parents, we need to give that same unconditional love and abundance of mercy to our children. Yes, just as God causes us to suffer for our mistakes, we need to set limits for our children. Yet, above everything, children need to know they are deeply loved by their parents and by the Lord.

Bryna succinctly brings this chapter to a close in the following scenario. I opened up the refrigerator one day and discovered some sort of a disaster within. Pulling out the mess, I asked, "Who did this?"

With a glint in her eye, Bryna responded, "Kids? Ya gotta love 'em."

I don't remember the disaster, but I do remember the laughter. She had it right! She was the only kid living at home at the time, since her sisters had moved into marriage.

Kids are messy. They leave muddy tracks on carpets and messes in the kitchen, and they are noisy, emotional, and needy! But they are huge blessings from God and we are so thankful for them.

Kids? Ya gotta love 'em!

Chapter 12

STRUGGLES

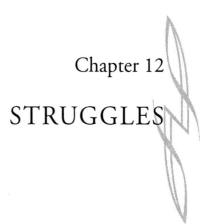

I AM NOT going to recount all the details of the black years following Bryna's hospitalizations. While in the hospital, she met some girls who showed her how to make herself vomit. Once free from the institution, she sought out drugs, which led to drug treatment at Remuda Ranch, a wonderful facility for her. Then she fell into an eating disorder along with cutting on herself. We cashed in all our retirement money so she could get help from a reputable eating disorder facility. She relapsed two weeks after coming home, never to be freed of it.

Those years of living with her eating disorder were extremely painful. We were on opposite sides of her disease. She had no desire to be rid of the eating disorder, and from our perspective, we saw only physical deterioration. It would have felt so good if we were on the same team, her and us rooting for a solution, and working together for her healing. But we were on opposing teams. She would thump her rib cage and I can still hear the noise in my memory. Her bones cracked as she walked down the hall. She passed out on some of her runs. I thought of her huge potential athletically when she was young and how I worked so hard to give her the best baby food. I thought of her strength in first grade at climbing up the rope hanging from the gymnasium ceiling. I thought of her delightful personality and all the potential locked inside her. We grieved over her failing health. We tried counseling treatment centers. It is so painful to watch your child get sicker when you know you have all the food necessary to give her physical health.

To those of you who have not had an eating disorder, I strongly advise you to never, ever, ever, ever allow yourself to buy laxatives or weight-reducing pills from the stores. It is a dangerously slippery slope from such an innocent purchase to being held captive with an eating disorder. Your whole life will soon revolve around satisfying the eating disorder. You will turn down social engagements connected with food, and you will become swallowed up in a lonely, painful battle. In hiding your secret world, you will find yourself imprisoned in the darkest of cells. Eating disorders kill. Satan will tell you that an eating disorder is a way of being in control of your world. That is a lie straight from hell. Bryna is testimony to the fact that eating disorders kill.

If you have an eating disorder, there is help for you, once you are determined to receive the help. It is a tough journey, but many have gone before you and have received healing. Your disease not only hurts you, it hurts everyone who loves you. And I am sure there are many more people who love you than you know. Get help. God has a life of great potential for you.

Being the parent of a child with an eating disorder is lonely. The causes driving the disease are largely not understood by our society, for it varies from person to person, and is a hard disease to explain. The root causes are similar to the root causes of alcohol and drug addictions. By keeping the disease a secret from others, because of the stigma attached to the disorder, parents further isolate themselves. There is the haunting thought, "Where did we go wrong?" Parents blame themselves, even though they don't know what they did to cause it. There is a temptation to run into a hole and hide.

I chose to run to God instead. Sometimes my heart was so heavy, I was afraid to go to church; afraid that I would break down in tears during the service. But I went anyway. Sometimes tears did escape my control, but always, I left thankful that I had come. Hearing God's Word, worshipping with a group of believers, brought healing to my famished soul.

Frequently I took off on prayer runs. Running and praying seems to be the style of communication that works best for me. I tried to be one of those "kneel beside the bed" people, but I didn't last long. However, once I ran halfway around my four-mile running loop, I was committed to the full course. No telephones or people interrupted the running prayers. And since I ran in one big loop, I didn't get lost. God had my undivided attention.

I often left on the prayer runs weighed down with problems, lifting feet that felt like cement blocks were attached. It didn't take long to start pouring out my heart before the Lord. After venting, I ran in silence, letting my mind drift to wherever it wanted to go, trusting God to direct my thinking. When we draw near to God, He draws near to us. What a privilege that we can turn to Him anytime, anywhere, and dressed in running clothes. He listened to me and He encouraged and strengthened me.

One time in particular I felt the root of bitterness begin to take hold in my heart. I could feel it physically. Anyone out there know what I mean? I said, "God, You let this one thing happen to Bryna, and the other bad thing, and now this. Where are You?" About ten running steps further God spoke into my mind, "I have a ministry for Bryna, not in spite of what has happened, but because of what has happened." My root of bitterness dissolved.

I don't know if this book is part of God's promise for Bryna's ministry or if you, the reader, are part of His promise. If you ever want to go on a prayer run in Gig Harbor, I will show you exactly where God dissolved my root of bitterness and gave me His promise for Bryna's ministry.

Near the end of my four-mile loop, a big hill looms before me. As I approach that hill, I usually tell God, "Thank you, God, for allowing the hills in my life. If it weren't for the hard times, I would never have known You as my loving Heavenly Father." So true.

When tragedy strikes; when life beats you up;
RUN TO GOD!
Grab your Kleenex and CHARGE TO CHURCH.

Chapter 13

SUNSHINE

I LOVE THE story of the paralyzed man who was unable on his own to make his way to Jesus. Jesus was preaching to a huge crowd that filled up a home in Capernaum and spilled outside the door. There was no room for a paralytic lying on a mat. His four friends, determined that he should be brought to Jesus, improvised a solution not befitting cultural norms. With the doorways blocked, they decided to go through the roof. That must have been a conversation stopper! The roof was probably made of a thick layer of clay, supported by mats of branches across wood beams. One of the friends must have been an engineer, because they lowered him down without spilling him off the mat. Talk about laying our problems at the feet of Jesus! There he was, at the feet of Jesus. Did Jesus just snap His fingers and heal the paralysis? No, He didn't. He first dealt with the inner turmoil of the man. "Son, your sins are forgiven." Then He told him, "Get up, take up your mat, and go home" (Mark 2:1–12).

Without his friends carrying his mat and lowering him through the roof, the man would not have seen Jesus or been healed. Without all the friends surrounding Bryna through the years, I can only imagine the terrors of her story. She had an enormous hedge of protection around her where people were the plants, and new plants continued to spring up. As with the paralytic, she needed to see Jesus and encounter His love. Some people were counselors in middle school and high school who poured out to Bryna both inside and outside school hours. They loved on her and steered her into truth and health. They dealt with the inner issues just as Jesus dealt with the paralytic's inner issues. Her high school teacher saw Bryna as a big bundle of potentiality. She never gave up on Bryna and pursued Bryna through the bumps in the road. One friend, who is not a pet lover, went on many dog walks with Bryna and delighted in conversing with her. These adults poured themselves out to Bryna. Youth workers, youth pastors and their wives, our pastor and his wife, my friends, prayer groups, all spent time with Bryna, listening, counseling, praying and witnessing a gradual healing.

When clouds of darkness rolled in, I reflected on that hedge of protection, which I earnestly prayed for, and my heart would be lifted. I did not walk this path alone, for friends surrounded us. I am so thankful for the friends who supported me with hugs and prayers, encouragement and advice.

Scriptures call us to love one another, pray for one another, counsel one another, and encourage one another. We are to reach out horizontally to one another as we reach up vertically to God. I am thankful for the horizontal community and I know a loving community delights the Lord. We also have to open up horizontally to let those around us know how they can help. Since help comes in various forms, through acts of service or conversations or quality time or hugs, people need to know how they can help.

One Saturday morning I put on my tennis shoes and headed out for a walk. However, the thought of walking alone suddenly felt depressing. "Please, Lord, help me find someone who wants to go on a walk and talk about anything other than my problems. I just want to laugh with a friend." I made a couple phone calls, with no success. Headed out once again, I grabbed the doorknob just when the phone rang. Running back, "It is someone wanting to go on a walk!" And it was.

A friend I had not seen for months joined me on a fun walk. "Thank you, Lord." I was not suicidal; there was no emergency in having that walk with a friend. But God gave me the present as if to say, "I am with you."

God gives us friends and hedges of protection as sunshine filtering through the clouds. Thank you, Lord.

> "The LORD is close to the brokenhearted
> and saves those who are crushed in spirit."
> —Psalm 34:18

Chapter 14

HOPE

"The Lord is good to those whose hope is in him,
to the one who seeks him."

—Lamentations 3:25

WE, MY FAMILY and friends, were seeking God for Bryna. Our hope was in God's care for Bryna. On the other hand, Bryna kept losing all hope. Starting out with being raped in the third grade by an older brother of a friend, and again numerous times by another person, and later by a taxicab driver in Guatemala, plus the involuntary hospitalizations, drugs, a learning disability, and an eating disorder, she wanted to quit living. Her first suicidal attempt was in the third grade with the Clorox. The next one was an attempt to drive off a cliff. Just as she was leaving at nine p.m., Tina from Florida, at midnight in her time zone, called Bryna. Who calls for conversation at midnight? Another time I clued in when she gave several presents away and exuded peace. Fortunately, her high school counselor bent the confidentiality rule, and her life was barely spared. We held an intervention, urging her to voluntarily seek hospitalization. At the conclusion of the meeting, she agreed to our proposal, excusing herself to the bathroom, and secretly drank the contents of her suicidal packet. When she was brought back from her close brush with death in the emergency room, she was angry with us for not letting her die.

In later years Bryna said with a glint in her eye, "It's no use trying to kill myself, because God always intervenes."

His intervention was our hope. And it did happen in an amazing way. While recovering in the hospital from the last suicidal attempt, Bryna was given choices for her next steps of healing. She decided to try a home in Texas, called Beauty For Ashes. Before committing herself to any treatment, she wanted to check it out first. If it looked promising, she would return to Washington State, pack her suitcases, and give it a try.

Hope and anxiety filled our hearts. Little did we know that she also packed her suicidal kit. If Beauty For Ashes turned out to not be a good fit, she intended to drink the contents of her kit on the way back in the plane, when no one could stop the effects by a quick trip to the emergency room.

At this time in her life, she hated Jesus because He was way too perfect, and she wanted to die and go to hell so that she could be with her friends. Anyone arguing with Bryna quickly learned that she could take the conversation where she wanted it to go. She should have been on a debate team, because she would have been a winner!

She and Tara, the director of Beauty For Ashes, had a lively discussion about hell and Jesus and who knows what else. On Sunday morning, they attended a Sunday school class taught by

Beth Moore, a captivating Bible teacher. It was on the subject of heaven and hell. (Where is God? He was right there in that class!) In the evening service, Beth Moore was again the speaker, continuing on with the same topic. By the end of the service, Bryna fell on her knees and was sobbing. She wanted Jesus in her life. She wanted to receive Him as her personal Savior. Beth questioned her motives, and Bryna expressed her reasons. She jumped on the plane the next morning, poured her suicidal kit down the toilet, and headed home to pack her bags.

On the trip back home, she talked to a passenger all about God, and shared experiences. And again, I don't know all that they talked about. But Bryna told me, "At the end of our trip, the lady thanked me for talking with her and said I was a big inspiration to her."

Bryna was changed. The talk about hating Jesus and wanting to go to hell never returned.

I wish her stay at Beauty For Ashes had eliminated the eating disorder, but it did not. However, Bryna began talking about the future for the first time. She allowed herself to have dreams and hope. So encouraging!

Bryna enrolled in a vocational school to pursue a para-educator degree. We worked together on that dream. Her teacher, Mrs. Write-Another-Paper, spewed out assignments, specializing in length and research. Writing was a lost art for Bryna, but speaking was her specialty. So we teamed up. She spoke and I typed frantically fast to keep up with her. Then we edited my gazillion typing errors and her thinking. We became a research paper factory. In addition to all the papers, Bryna had to take algebra. With my background as a calculus teacher, I planned to coach her on the side. A week into the course, I was totally unprepared for her reaction. "What the heck are all these letters doing in a math course? Math is supposed to be with numbers, not letters." She ranted and raved for three days about the illogic of sticking letters in a math class. My answers sounded so feeble compared to her wailing. I'm saying, Mr. Psychiatrist, try arguing with Bryna on algebra.

We made it through the course. The next big hurdle was getting a job. She interviewed with a group of people who all wanted a job. They were seated around a big oval table. As questions were asked, each person in the group had to give their answer. Tense!

Bryna came home with the report, "I know I did not get the job. But at least I know better what kind of questions to think about." We were on the way out the door to go to a Target store when Bryna answered the phone. It was a very short conversation. After finding my purse, we headed again for the door when I asked her,

"So who called?"

"Oh, it was the school."

"So, what did they say?"

She reported calmly, and with no emotion, "They said I got the job."

"GOT THE JOB?" I was screaming. I ran after her! We went crazy!! Bazerko crazy!!!

"What was all this stuff about not getting the job?"

"I don't know, Mom. Really. There was another lady there that I was sure had the best answers. I can't believe I got the job."

Bryna had compiled an amazing portfolio and landed a real job as a real para-educator in the Tacoma Public Schools. How thrilling! She worked with a small group of children suffering from autism. She poured herself into those children, and knew how to relate with them, and genuinely loved them. She loved her job and loved the people she was working with. Her life had purpose!

I attended a field trip with her class and chaperoned one boy, who I continually lost. It was so scary losing him in crowds of children. I watched Bryna move with ease and competence as she directed a much more difficult child. I felt like a porcupine in a fish tank, completely out of my element. I saw true love as I watched Bryna and her coworkers love on these children, whom others often criticized for being not like everyone else. The pain and trials she had faced in her life groomed her for being sensitive to the hurting.

I will never forget the thrill of seeing her teaching evaluation. There were about twelve categories where she could receive a score from 1 to 5. With the exception of two 4s, the rest were 5s. One 4 was for attendance, where she missed two days of school. The other 4 was for professional development, where she had not taken a course since her graduation. Her performance was clearly outstanding. We danced! We shouted!

In fact, the principal encouraged her to continue college training. She recognized in Bryna a talent for working with special education children, and she recommended that Bryna earn her teaching degree. Apparently Mr. Psychiatrist forgot to talk to the principal! I'm laughing. The psychiatrist had only the testing tools he had been given, and he had to speak from a statistical reference point. I don't really have a grudge against him, probably wouldn't throw a rotten tomato at him; if I did, it would be a small one! But I do rejoice in the success and honor

Bryna earned in the workplace. And I thank God that He kept thwarting the suicidal attempts.

Her dreams grew. She wanted to buy a two-bedroom house and take in a foster child. She talked future and we were encouraged, except for the monster eating disorder, lurking in the shadows.

> Thank you, God, for bestowing on Bryna
> a crown of beauty instead of ashes.

Chapter 15

RESTORATION

"And the God of all grace,
who called you to his eternal glory in Christ,
after you have suffered a little while,
will himself restore you
and make you strong, firm and steadfast."

—1 Peter 5:10

DO YOU LOVE the above verse? So beautiful and so true!
God delights to restore us. While He was restoring Bryna,
and building up Lynell, Stacey, and Teryl, He was also restoring
Dave and me.

We were over-the-top in love with each other forty-three
years ago and knew that marriage was the first step in living
happily ever after. Totally oblivious to buried hurts, we climbed
mountains, canoed rivers, and folk danced with joy. However,
life has its way of burbling up unresolved issues. As problems
surfaced, we tried solutions that did not work. Although we

treasure many fun memories with each other and with our children, we also experienced disconnect in our relationship. Marriage, for me, was hard work. It became hard work with almost no fun. Dave, on the other hand, felt like things were going well. We did not operate as a team of two in facing the hardships of life. Our issues hurt not only us but our children. Hurting people hurt others. How our girls became the beautiful women and mothers and wives they are today is credit only to God. He does have the power to make all things beautiful.

Wounded deeply in childhood, Dave made some unwise choices that adversely affected my well-being. We sought counseling and found new paths, only to sink back into the pit again. Eight years ago I initiated our separation.

Even though we had scriptural support for divorce, I did not know what to do. I believed God could heal, and I knew statistics were against us. Dave's choices were life threatening and I wanted to be alive for my grandchildren. This period of separation was the most tormenting time of my life. Suddenly, I was in the driver's seat, and my decisions would affect the lives of all my family members, including those grandbabies not yet born. Dave wanted our marriage to continue. I did not know what to do.

There is a time to divorce. Although God hates divorce, He also opposes abuse. Sometimes God restores through divorce, sometimes through marriage.

Brilliantly (I say this facetiously), I resolved to go through a forty-day fast—not from food, but from tormenting myself with questions about what I should do. More than anything, I passionately wanted to do what was right in the sight of the Lord. I soaked in scripture; I went on prayer walks; I delighted in the presence of the Lord. And I did not worry about what I should do, for I believed at the end of forty days, God would make that clear. I checked the days off on a calendar.

At the end of my fast, I waited before God. Nothing! "Are You out there, God?" Nothing. No lightning from the skies. No sign popping down from heaven, saying "Take this trail." Nothing. I tried the counselor route. Some people saw potential for change; others saw warnings of disaster. One Christian counselor talked with me for an hour and ended up yelling at me, "How can you be so blind? You need to divorce; this is a hopeless relationship." I left that session, still questioning in my heart, "What should I do?" I wanted to do what was right in the sight of the Lord. I started divorce proceedings; my heart was in turmoil.

Five months into the separation, Dave invited me to attend the National Institute of Marriage, founded by Greg Smalley along with Bob Paul and Mark Pyatt. Should I go? If I were to error in making my decision, I decided I would more easily live with the error of choosing to go rather than the error of refusing to go.

The application form, eleven pages, took a while to prepare. One question asked, on a scale of one to ten, ten being the strongest desire, how strongly did I wish to remain married? I wrote in zero.

The marriage intensive was definitely intensive. Grouped with three other couples, we worked from eight in the morning until five p.m. Our leaders turned the environment into a safe and loving place for all of us. On the morning of our last day, I took off at five thirty in the morning, running, crying, and praying in the rain. I still did not know what to do. "Please, Lord, help me."

Later in the morning Dave shared an incident that reflected the rejection he felt in his young years. When he was about ten years old, he had an argument in the car with his mom, who stopped the car and ordered him to get out. She drove on without him.

Holding up a teddy bear to represent Dave, the counselor asked him, "If you were a boy walking down the street, and you saw another boy stranded on the street, what would you say to him?"

"I would tell him I am sorry for what happened and things are going to be OK."

"If you were a grown man walking down the street, and you saw a boy stranded on the street, what would you do?"

"I would put my arm around him, and tell him things are going to be OK."

"If you are back to being that little boy, and if Jesus came down the street, what would He do?"

Dave couldn't talk. As he imagined being a young boy again, all the feelings of rejection and unworthiness, feelings of being unloved and unwanted, boiled up inside. Tears spilled down his face, and sobs broke out. His shoulders were shaking and his head was buried in his hands. We all waited silently until he finally managed to get the words out.

"He would put His arms around me and tell me He loves me."

We were silent. I watched his shoulders shake and felt in my spirit that something significant was happening. The lie of rejection was being uprooted by the truth of Jesus' love.

By the end of the day, I told Dave I wanted to give our marriage a try. I knew I was standing on shaky ground and acting against all logic in saying "yes." I had a list of what needed to happen before making this decision. None of those things had happened at this point. But I had seen God's hand move that morning in a way I never anticipated.

Change does not happen suddenly; it is a process. I knew how to almost survive in a dysfunctional marriage, but I didn't know how to suddenly be a team person. I pushed Dave's buttons and he did not respond as he used to. He reacted with patience and kindness, rather than anger. I had spent many years carefully avoiding the punching of his buttons, and now I was punching more than ever. He wanted to pray with me; I wanted to run the opposite direction. His change required me to change from being solo pilot in my own sphere of responsibilities to being copilot. My trust level was stuck at zero. How does one make all those changes? The answer is: Slowly, oh, so slowly.

It has been nearly eight years since we decided in August 2005 to reunite, and what a journey. We are more in love now than we ever had been. I found out that people don't marry soulmates. They become soulmates! There is no way to become soulmates until you can go through the bumps and thrills of life together. It is a process.

In times past, whenever I heard married people say, "We are soul mates," I looked on with envy, wishing I could have married a "soul mate." Now I realize that we married people all have a chance at being married to our soul mate without having to change mates! We don't marry soul mates; we become soul mates.

I would like to share one particular skill we learned in attending the marriage institute, which has been instrumental in changing our communication. For years we had attempted to communicate with the "I feel ..." statements rather than the attack statements that always start out as "You ..." But we could turn any "I feel" statement into an attack statement:

"I feel like you rejected me when ..."

"Well, I feel like your anger was unjustified when ..."

And the buttons get pushed like crazy.

Sometimes we would be in an exchange where one person slipped onto a detour around the subject, bringing up issues off track and diving into other pits of conflict. Dave masterly sabotaged word pictures that I tried using in communication. We were masters at dysfunctional communication.

For all you married people who have achieved marriage oneness, you have full permission to laugh at my explanation below as being common-sense simple. It seems too simple to write out, yet it has had a profound effect on our marriage.

This is the deal: We have to take turns at being speaker. (I warned you that this sounds kindergarten simple!) Usually, I, being the most emotionally distraught, get to be first speaker. When it is my turn, I speak out the issue with all my feelings. I express how I am feeling and the truth I see. I bear in mind that the goal of the conversation is not to prove one of us right and the other wrong, nor to prove my spouse is my enemy. The goal is oneness. After I speak, then Dave is to state back in his own words what he heard. This never seems to agree with what I think I said. So, I then clarify those issues. Dave may have a tendency to try to defend himself, but that is against the rules. Speaker two cannot defend himself until speaker one feels totally understood. We usually go through three or four rounds of my expressing and him interpreting until I feel totally understood.

At this point, Dave becomes the speaker. He speaks out about his feelings and hurts and point of view, and I repeat back what I thought I heard. If I heard wrong, he then gets the floor to speak until he thinks he has said enough for me to understand his message. It is then my turn to tell him what I heard. I cannot defend myself. We take turns being speaker until we both feel understood and validated, falling naturally into each other's arms and rejoicing over unity. It works! We don't have to force ourselves to express forgiveness or obey any other hard rules. It just flows so peacefully. This is our method of escape from the button-pushing cycles that led only to further discontent.

Another truth that has been seared in our consciences is, "Our spouse is not our enemy." When life throws stress bumps, we don't need to hurl "enemy attack grenades" at our spouse. Marriage is a team sport!

God is a God of second chances. He understands our hurts and pain. He restores.

> The Lord is my shepherd, I lack nothing.
>   He makes me lie down in green pastures,
> he leads me beside quite waters,
>   he refreshes my soul.

Thank you, God, for not giving up on my family. You worked powerfully in all our lives and You restored gradually our relationships with each other. You restored our souls.

Chapter 16

GRIEF

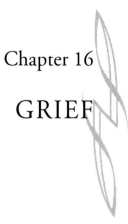

"Even though I walk through the valley
of the shadow of death,
I will fear no evil, for you are with me."

—Psalm 23:4

LOOKING FORWARD, WE ask, "Where are You, God?" Looking backward, we see His handprints everywhere.

Stacey, who lived in North Carolina, was pregnant with her fourth child. I booked airline tickets so that I could hopefully be present when the baby was born. Unfortunately, my trip conflicted with Bryna's spring vacation. To rectify the problem, we planned an ocean trip with Bryna during Presidents' weekend in February. Teryl's family of five with their little dog, Mortie, joined our family of three, with Bryna's dog, Zoey. The weather was sunny and warm, defying the typical cold February temperatures. We ran in the sand, played in the waves, and threw balls for the dogs. Never have we taken so many photos.

In fact, Dave and I are masters of packing cameras and never taking them out of their cases. Bryna was happy and free, her hair blowing in the wind, as she picked up two year old Ashley and whirled her around. Always planning fun activities for children, Bryna bought rubber boots for Ashley to play in. She and the boys drew pictures in the sand with their long sticks, and they jumped waves. We all had such a wonderful time. It was the perfect trip.

Back home, Bryna's legs swelled with edema, the first sign of a downward spiral. She did visit her eating disorder doctor, whom she had not seen for several years. Bryna forged ahead with school, in spite of her fatigue. A gastrointestinal virus slammed her into bed. Recovery was slow. She consented to an urgent care visit, where they claimed she had an ear infection, for which they wrote a prescription. No mention was made of her lack of weight. Bryna regained her strength. One week before I was scheduled to leave for North Carolina, I commented,

"Bryna, you have been off your eating disorder regime for a few days. You could turn this thing around."

"I don't want to turn it around."

"If you don't turn it around, it is going to kill you."

"Get used to it."

I got up and left the room. I was furious inside. I didn't even know at whom I was angry. Bryna and I, for once, were on the same team when we walked into urgent care. It felt so good to be on her team. But the ugly eating disorder monster kept getting in the way and pushing us apart. He was destroying her and I couldn't stop him. He was in my house and I wanted him out. In anger, I banged out on the computer,

"If Bryna's funeral is on the day Stacey goes into labor, I am going to be with Stacey. I am for the living and not for the dead."

I am not proud of that statement, but I am honestly telling you what happened.

Bryna returned to school, and one week later, I flew to North Carolina. On Thursday night, the day before Stacey would be induced, Bryna and Dave looked up airline trips that she might take during her spring break. She had one last day of school before break. After looking at possibilities for flights to California and Florida, she said,

"I'm really tired, Dad. One more day and I have spring break."

That was their last conversation together.

Early in the morning, Dave saw her bathroom light on, and walked in to see if she was up. He discovered her on the floor, called 911, and desperately administered artificial resuscitation. Even though he had taught the course, he couldn't do it for his own daughter without the medics helping him over the phone. Bryna was already dead. He called me at the hospital, where I sat beside Stacey, who was waiting to be induced. "Bryna died," Dave reported with no preamble, being in a state of shock.

"Bryna died?" not believing I was hearing him correctly.

"Bryna died," he repeated.

"Bryna died," I echoed.

Those words I had typed on the computer suddenly became reality. What do I do? "I am for the living, not the dead." I needed to be with Stacey. She needed to have the baby. I thought of the grandchildren I had not seen yet. We had planned a hot dog party after Stacey's baby was to be born. Do I leave now for home in Washington? Do I stay in North Carolina with Stacey? What about the grandchildren? They just lost their auntie who loved them dearly. Does their Nana take off too, without seeing them? "I am for the living." God prepared a characteristically indecisive mom, in advance, for making an important decision.

Dave and I decided I should stay one night, get some sleep, and fly out in the morning. The plan seemed reasonable in the moment, but turned out to be exceptionally hard for both of us. There would be no sleep for me and Dave's suffering would be intense. He sacrificed big time for me.

I walked out into the hospital hall, stunned, in a fog, passed by the nurses' station, and numbly commented as I walked by, "My daughter just died."

I was in shock and continued walking right on past the nurses' station. Unknown to me, nurses flew to Stacey's room, thinking she had passed away.

I don't remember where my walk took me, probably to the restroom, but when I returned to Stacey's room, nurses were telling her that she could wait another day to be induced. She looked at me and said,

"I really want to have this baby today."

"I totally agree with you, Stacey. I also want you to have this baby today."

I determined right then that I would be joy in Stacey's room and I would take my tears and diarrhea outside her room. When emotion swelled up inside, I would take leave. When things settled down, I was back with Stacey. Nurses helped me by allowing me to use a lounge for hospital staff only. Someone on staff sat with me and helped me think through the next steps. Likewise, people were surrounding Dave in our home.

I felt like a pendulum swinging from being a mother to Stacey and wanting to be involved in every step of the delivery process to a heap of tangled emotions in the hallways. Lynell found babysitting help and soon arrived in the hospital parking lot. I remember running toward her and embracing each other as if we were grabbing onto a lifeline.

Little Joshua was born at two in the afternoon. Stacey had her baby and we celebrated as much as we could. I had a headache, and left with Lynell soon after, while Stacey lay in bed trying to wrap her head around gaining a baby boy and losing a sister all in the same day.

The hot dog party sort of happened. The children did not comprehend the little we tried to share. I went to bed and could not sleep. Lynell and I wept in front of the computer as we read loving comments from Bryna's friends. It was good that we had time to grieve together, the result of Dave sacrificing time he could have spent with me.

From the moment Dave called me to say, "Bryna died," a black PowerPoint slide appeared in my mind with shaky white writing saying, "Bryna Died." That slide was with me all day and all night, and the white writing vibrated.

I tried various mind tricks for falling asleep, but nothing worked. The black slide prevailed. At five thirty in the morning, after no sleep, I prepared for my airline trip home.

God went before me. Having a pacemaker, I was required to have a pat down rather than go through the metal detectors. When I confided my reasons for flying to the security guard, she stopped in the middle of my pat down, hugged me, and offered condolences, before continuing on with the pat down. Her embrace spoke volumes. On the flight, I sat next to a young woman who opened up to me. I told her very little about Bryna, and she returned with, "I had a sister with an eating disorder. Your daughter's death was not your fault."

Her words were a soothing ointment for my troubled heart. So where was God when I was assigned a seat next to someone who compassionately understood eating disorders? Our conversation around eating disorders was brief, for my pain was too great for a lengthy discussion. She spoke words of encouragement and gave me some snacks she brought in her purse. We laughed and ate crackers together. I am so thankful my seat assignment placed me next to her, for she ministered to my soul.

Bryna's bedroom and our bedroom were on opposite ends of the house, and connected by our kitchen. I feared walking into the house. After climbing the stairs from our garage, I had to pass through the kitchen to get to our bedroom. The kitchen brought too many memories of Bryna and me together. It was our hang-out spot. I wasn't sure I could look at the kitchen again, knowing our hanging-out days were over.

Fortunately, a huge bouquet of purple and white flowers on our kitchen table caught me by surprise, distracting me from my fears. I focused on the flowers as I quickly slid by the kitchen table into our hallway leading into our bedroom. Do flowers minister to people? Yes, they do!

We crashed into bed, so thankful to be together in our pain.

Do you see God's hand? We would not have created the February ocean trip had it not been for the airline conflict with Bryna's spring vacation. She died before her spring vacation started. Had it not been for the ocean trip, we would not have had all those photos where Bryna was so happy and so free. We would not have had the happy memories of being together as family on the beach. God was there when we were planning trips. Bryna never wanted me to see her dead body. Each planned suicide was carefully crafted so that I would not see her body. I am thankful, hard as it was for Dave, that I did not see her dead in our house. I do not want that memory. I know it was so, so, so hard for Dave. But I was spared. I thank God selfishly for sparing me. I thank God for Dave's courage and for his care for me in providing the extra sleep that never happened. Dave gave his all for me when I was stricken down. I thank God for bringing our marriage together so we could lean on each other for this hard time in our life. I thank Him for giving all of us time for healing relationships before Bryna was taken. I thank God, our loving Heavenly Father, for allowing Bryna to experience honor and respect and success in the workplace before taking her home. I thank You, Lord, I will get to see her again. Meanwhile, I am grateful she is in the care of Jesus. And thank you, God, for the three beautiful daughters we still have. Oh, and God, this is silly, but thank you for Zoey, who seems like a small piece of Bryna that is still alive here on earth. My loving on Zoey feels like I am giving a little love back to Bryna.

And Bryna, I'm not "over it." None of us are. You have a place in our hearts, and always will. We miss you.

Where is God when everything goes wrong?
He goes before us, comes alongside us, and lifts us up.

Chapter 17

LOVING KINDNESS
AND MERCY

"Surely goodness and love will follow
me all the days of my life."

—Psalm 23:6

S LEEP IS A gift, and after thirty-six hours with no sleep for
me since Bryna died, and only two or three hours for Dave,
we were comatose! At five thirty on Sunday morning, we were
brutally awakened by a cat fight. Seriously? Our two cats, which
rarely fought, chose this morning, of all mornings, to shake up
the house. My black PowerPoint mental slide with "Bryna Died"
came back to life as Dave lumbered out of bed.

"So, do we go to church today?"

"I don't know."

Through the years I pushed myself to church when I least
felt like going, not because I was trying to please God or earn
brownie points, but because, deep down, I knew I needed God.
I would leave for church, depressed, and return encouraged.
Soaking in God's presence always changes us.

But what about two days after your daughter has died? Before a memorial service?

Wide awake, despite our short sleep, Dave, robot style, took his morning shower. Brain-dead, I followed. Before we knew what was happening, we were dressed for church, for the early service. We are usually lucky to be ready for the second service. I don't remember much about that strange morning, but I do remember feeling like a tin soldier in the church pew. Our presence definitely caused a spirit of uneasiness. Fifteen minutes into the service, our pastor stopped everything and asked the congregation to surround the Johnsons and pray for them. Tears are flowing as I write this. That prayer meant everything to us. The comfort of the Lord was showered upon us through His people.

During our worship songs, God gave me the most beautiful gift. I saw Bryna standing so tall and straight, her face radiant, with her big smile. Her feet, not touching the ground, hung gracefully as she was suspended about a foot off the ground. Jesus was standing beside her with His left arm snugly wrapped around her waist, and His right arm extended upwards in a "praise the Lord" posture. The black mental slide was gone! Replacing the "Bryna Died" slide, this vision captured my heart. Tears streamed down my face as I felt the holiness of the moment.

The vision of Bryna being held by Jesus did not leave me. It was in front of me when I talked to people, when I was alone, wherever I was. It stayed with me constantly in my waking hours. I could be talking about cooking hamburgers, and the vision of Bryna would remain in front of me. Many months later it would come and go. Today, four years later, I can recall it clearly. In those early weeks without Bryna's presence, it was always with me.

Did we do the right thing in going to church? We did! Glory hallelujah! We are tempted, as hurting people, to run from God when we need Him most. We want to come to Him when we feel "put together," not when we feel like we are falling apart, when we need Him more than ever. Sin and pain and death are in the world. Bad things happen to good people. We run from God when He wants to hold us in His arms.

The next week friends brought huge meals for us as our house filled up with all our children and grandchildren. Lynell and Teryl planned a beautiful memorial service. Stacey, still in recovery from giving birth, flew out with little five-day-old Joshua. Her doctor had to give written permission for her to fly with a newborn baby.

Lynell and Teryl made the reception room look like a wedding reception, with the pink-and-brown polka-dot cups and Bryna's favorite candies spilled out on the table. The church is the bride of Christ; Bryna graduated to heaven; Bryna is no longer with us. Whatever we were commemorating—wedding, graduation, her passing—it was beautiful.

Deaconesses in our church helped with decorations and reception foods. When they learned that pink was Bryna's favorite color, they actually tore down some of their decorations and redecorated with pink.

The compassion people lavished upon us through the meals, gifts, cards, and attendance at the memorial service was overwhelming. We felt truly loved upon. Four years later I am saying to some of the memorial plants, "Come on! You can do it. You can bloom just one more time."

On my first time alone in the car, I turned on the radio with Chris Tomlin singing "I Will Rise." Oh my goodness, I had to pull the car off the road and weep hysterically as he sang. It was an awesome song, which I had never heard before. Such hope. To think of Bryna with Jesus and singing praises ... I copied the lyrics below:

I Will Rise

By Chris Tomlin

There's a peace I've come to know
Though my heart and flesh may fail
There's an anchor for my soul
I can say "It is well"
Jesus has overcome
And the grave is overwhelmed
The victory is won
He is risen from the dead
And I will rise when He calls my name
No more sorrow, no more pain
I will rise on eagles' wings
Before my God fall on my knees
And rise
I will rise
There's a day that's drawing near
When this darkness breaks to light
And the shadows disappear
And my faith shall be my eyes
Jesus has overcome
And the grave is overwhelmed
The victory is won
Jesus is risen from the dead
And I will rise when He calls my name,

No more sorrow, no more pain
I will rise on eagles' wings
Before my God fall on my knees
And rise
I will rise
And I hear the voice of many angels sing,
"Worthy is the Lamb"
And I hear the cry of every longing heart,
"Worthy is the Lamb"
And I will rise when He calls my name,
No more sorrow, no more pain
I will rise on eagles' wings
Before my God fall on my knees
And rise
I will rise

Bryna no longer has pain or sorrow. Victory is won. She is alive with Jesus. In God's mercy He took her. Her personal pains, her pain over seeing her last counselor die, her pain of losing several other friends in death, they were big. But God took her after relationships had been restored, after Bryna experienced success and purpose in the workplace, after she found a new relationship with Jesus. He took her in mercy. And He took her with loving kindness extended to all of us adjusting to our loss. If I had to sum up my first year without Bryna in three words, I would say I was consumed by the "mercy and loving kindness" of the Lord.

There is no way I can answer the "why" questions. We miss her deeply. She was so fun. Walking into the Target store my first time without her was so difficult. It still is difficult. I miss that girl. Her decorated nails, the pink coat she wore, her cute hairstyle, her telling me I have my pant legs stuck inside my socks, her crazy humor, all the things she did to help me with my chores … I miss her.

I hear her laughing when I complained that the chips she bought didn't even taste good.

"You ate them? They're dog treats!"

She thought it was hilarious that the cat we were taking to the vet peed all over me when I took the cat from her arms as she was getting out of the car.

And she laughed uproariously when I innocently opened a greeting card that made a "meow" noise so real that our cat climbed me like a tree to attack the imaginary cat in the card. I was bleeding to death and she was bending over with laughter.

We miss your laughter, Bryna. You left a hole that only you can fill.

To some extent, we grieved fifteen years while she struggled through life. Maybe that made it easier for us after Bryna actually left. I don't know. Every death is different and everyone grieves differently. Some people need hugs; others do not want the hugs, nor want to be asked about how they are doing. Flowers minister to some, coffee dates to others, motorcycle rides to others.

Zoey is a perfect example of diversity in grieving. After a couple weeks, she stopped watching out the window for Bryna's arrival and went through a week of intense diarrhea. Now there's a style I hope most people will not copy! It did last for only one week and has never in six years come again. Yahoo! I've never seen her cry, but she kept disappearing into Bryna's room, where she scooted under Bryna's bed. She is big and the space is small, so there was no way I could drag her out. Calling her didn't work.

But when I stuck my head under the bed and talked softly to her, she came out of hiding. I buried my head in her fur and told her, "I am so sorry, Zoey. I know you miss Bryna. We all miss her. I love you. We are going to get through this."

Her tail wagged and we went on with life. Hugs worked for her; motorcycle rides are not one of her love languages. After several grieving spells under the bed, she no longer goes even near Bryna's room.

Grief comes in waves. You are innocently spraying Windex on the window, and wham, a tidal wave of crying strikes. When this happens, don't stop the wave. Have no fear, the wave will end. Ride it to the fullest. Go to the depths of your pain; let the tears come and the cries bellow. Cry with all you have until the wave is gone. After the wave, there is peace, and maybe even joy. Sometimes the waves will come in like a tropical storm. Other times a single wave will hit. There is healing in the waves. Let them come. Otherwise, there is danger of becoming stuck in your grief. Even though the waves will eventually come farther and farther apart, they will probably never stop.

Give yourself permission to laugh between the waves. Remember: **experiencing joy does not require the absence of pain.** If it did, we would all be in trouble. Pain and joy coexist. The sunset fills the skies in beauty while someone is dying in the hospital. Give yourself permission to experience joy while going through the grieving process. Having fun does not mean that you love the missing person less than you should. It is OK to eat an ice cream cone.

Desiring my girls to know, although I grieved deeply over missing Bryna, there was room in my heart to love them, Dave and I planned a "girls" trip and flew our three daughters to

Florida for an Eastern Caribbean cruise with me only six months after Bryna's passing. To hug, and laugh, and feast together was great therapy.

We have also returned several times to Bryna's beach, claiming happy memories, rather than allowing grief to manifest itself in producing fears of tears. Instead, the tears of remembrances console us in knowing how deeply we loved Bryna. We watch Zoey run after the seagulls, her black chow tail held high in the air with happiness, and we thank God for the many blessings.

Go to God. He understands your pain better than you do, and wants to shower you with His loving kindness, for He cares about the details of your life.

> Bryna, we love you.
> Precious daughter,
> Cherished sister,
> Beloved auntie,
> Beautiful friend,
> We shall see you again!

Chapter 18

HEAVEN'S DOOR

T HE ANGEL OF the LORD encamps around those who fear him, and he delivers them," as written in Psalm 34:7. I had this verse posted on my kitchen bulletin board for years. It is so reassuring to reflect upon the security with which the Lord surrounds His people. Just so we are all on the same page, the fear of the Lord mentioned in the above verse refers to our reverencing God by trusting and obeying Him. In the remaining pages of this book, I will share two stories of Rickieanne Bleistein and Sue that have been a huge encouragement to me in facing Bryna's passing. HUGE ENCOURAGEMENT!

Rickie, youth leader for our high school church group, and I met with rangers to plan a four-day hiking trip along the Wonderland Trail on Mount Rainier. Rob, youth pastor, headed up our group as we left Longmire for our eleven-mile trek to the nearest camping spot on a river. Eleven mountain miles are quite different than eleven street miles. We nearly had a mutiny on the ship when some of our boys wanted to camp on the rocky face of a mountain, rather than forge ahead to the designated spot. We needed to be by a river for our water supply, and hikers were only to camp in designated places.

The first day was a bit exhausting, but we made it. I remember lying down in my tent, feeling like every bone in my body was screaming out in pain. By morning, amazing to me, I felt great.

The Wonderland Trail is ninety-three miles long as it encircles Mount Rainier. It would be lovely if the trip could stay at a constant elevation. But instead, it goes miles down to rivers and up the other sides, over and over again. The views are spectacular and the hiking is exhilarating.

Rickie, not overly fond of her freeze-dried dinner she sampled the night before, dove into her bowl of oatmeal. After breakfast, we crossed the river where we had camped and climbed slowly up the opposite side. The morning sun beat down on us as we labored with our packs. Rickie delighted in the scenic views and stopped several times to inhale the beauty. And then I saw her stumble. Hot and sweaty like the rest of us, the expression on her face made me wonder if she was all right. We had climbed up the worst part of the canyon and found a place in the shade for rest and trail snacks. Rickie's skin was freezing cold and she was shivering in spite of the intense heat. I put a solar blanket around her and gave her sips of an electrolyte drink. We urged her to let us take her pack, but, sweet as she is, there is stubbornness inside her belonging to the best of mules. She was hiking and she was going to carry her pack. However, when she tried to put it on upside down, Rob grabbed it and added it to his pack.

We were hiking back in the days before cell phones were invented. No, it was not in the covered-wagon days. Rob hiked on ahead with some of our faster people, while I hiked right behind Rickie, stopping her every ten minutes for another electrolyte drink. Rickie continued tripping and stumbling along the trail. We traversed steep slopes where slipping could end up in a dangerous fall. I continually prayed, "Please, Lord, keep her feet on the trail. Give her Your endurance."

Her pace gradually quickened as we trekked onward. Throughout the day, I kept stopping her every ten minutes for more fluids. Finally, at four in the afternoon, our next riverside camping spot was a welcome sight. While the rest of us were anxious to get dinner cooked, Rickie's sole desire was to lie down for a nap. We quickly put up her tent and made her comfortable. After helping others with getting their tents up and boiling water for our freeze-dried dinners, I checked on Rickie. With the afternoon sun beating down on her tent, Rickie lay inside, freezing cold. She was shaking with cold. As we piled three sleeping bags around her, I urged her to eat.

"I don't want to eat; I just want to sleep."

"Rickie, you can't keep hiking if you can't eat."

"It is my heart's desire to hike. I will eat."

She had so many symptoms of hypothermia, which had almost taken my life in my canoeing days. I read about a case where three men fell off a boat into the Atlantic Ocean. When they were finally rescued and brought back on board, they delighted in eating hot bowls of soup in the galley. Within an hour, all three men died of heart attacks. Apparently, they were so cold that the hot soup caused parts of their body to thaw out too fast for other parts. Even though my scientific understanding of what exactly happened to the three sailors is lacking, I knew I did not want the soup I prepared for Rickie to be too hot. I dipped my finger into the soup, waiting for it to get near body temperature. That procedure was probably not necessary, but I didn't want to kill my friend with a bowl of soup.

She drank the soup and collapsed into her sleeping bag. Returning to her tent again, I felt her hands and they were still freezing cold. Looking back, I should have crawled into the sleeping bag with her and shared the warmth of my body.

I opened up my Bible and began reading out loud to her and praying for her.

"Blessed is he who has regard for the weak; the Lord delivers him in times of trouble" (Psalm 41:1).

"Lord, Rickie has a heart for the weak; they are her life. She continually pours out to high school kids; she reaches out to the hurting. We lift her up to You, oh Lord. Deliver her, we pray. Restore her."

"The Lord will sustain him on his sickbed and restore him from his bed of illness" (Psalm 41:3).

"Oh Lord, our Heavenly Father, Rickie needs Your hand of healing. She is here, lying before You, restore her."

I prayed and read scriptures for about half an hour. Laura, her youngest daughter, sat beside me. At about seven p.m., we heard her mumble into the sleeping bag,

"I'm not afraid to die."

"I know you are not afraid to die. But Rickie, Bob (her husband with multiple sclerosis) needs you. He needs you, Rickie. And Greg, he needs you, Rickie. Greg needs you. Tasha, Rickie, she needs you. Tasha needs you. And Laura, she is sitting right here with us. She needs you, Rickie, she needs you."

Rickie did not say anything. At 7:10 p.m., I felt her hands, and they were hot! HOT! They were hot for the first time since her tripping in the morning. I cautiously spoke with Rob.

"Rob, her hands are hot for the first time. She might make it. I don't know if she is going to pull through, but her hands are hot."

Rob had been poring over maps, trying to figure out the best way to get medical help for Rickie. He had located a ranger station on his map that was only five miles away. When he asked which youth might want to accompany him, Teryl eagerly volunteered. She was so afraid that Rickie was dying. She ran down to the river to "get a drink," but actually went down to cry where no one could see her. They gathered together one sleeping bag, a flashlight, map, solar blanket, a couple pop tarts, and trail food, and took off running. Having attended a summer cross-country track camp with teammates from high school, Teryl was in excellent shape. Rob later told us he could barely keep up with her! They left about 7:30 p.m. and ran nonstop to the ranger station. Running five miles of mountain miles is much harder than city miles. And they ran after a full day of hiking with packs. Unfortunately, the ranger doors were locked and no one was there. Due to a forest fire in Chelan, many of the rangers were forced to leave their stations. Devastated, they tried sleeping until daylight. Teryl, in the warm sleeping bag, woke up to the sound of Rob's teeth chattering under his solar blanket. They rearranged themselves so her sleeping-bag-encased legs were slung over on top of Rob, giving him enough warmth that he could get a little sleep. As soon as daylight approached, they sprang into action once again. Teryl and Rob, hiking with our youth group on the second day and continuing during the night on their own, hiked a total of twenty-three mountain miles. They arrived at the Mowich ranger station at eleven a.m. in the morning.

Meanwhile back at camp, Rickie, although listless, retained warmth in her hands. Laura, afraid to give herself permission to sleep, came to my tent at midnight.

"I think my mom is dying."

"Laura, she is lying still. I think the sleep is going to be good for her."

Fortunately, Rickie made it through the night, and got up in the morning with "I am ready to hike."

"Rickie, you are in no shape to hike. We have a plan for getting help."

"But it is my heart's desire to hike."

"Some of us are going to hike out on a logging road where we can meet up with help, while others wait with you."

"I am going with you."

"You need to stay here."

"I am going."

The mule within her had spoken once again.

Though the logging road was basically level, I watched Rickie as she lumbered along, pushing hard. At one point, we all stopped to take a trail food break in the shade. Rickie sat down in the hot sun, right where she had been walking.

"Rickie, do you really want to be sitting in the sun?"

"No, I guess I don't."

"Why don't you come over here into the shade?"

She gladly joined us in the shade. It was obvious that her logical thinking skills were still not quite functioning.

A ranger, who had been in communication with another ranger alerted by Rob and Teryl, met us on the way. He took Rickie and me into his truck while our group waited for Rob and Teryl to drive cars back to them. Teryl, who did not have her license yet, was driving! I am glad I did not know she was driving.

First-aid personnel quizzed us about everything, and praised us for having Rickie drink the electrolyte concoction every ten minutes. Hearing our details, they said several times that she exhibited all the signs of a potential fatality.

After the interrogations and kindness of the rangers and first-aid responders, we stood alongside the road, waiting for our group to come for us. Rickie turned to me and said,

"Marlys, there is more to the story that I need to tell you. If it weren't for you, I wouldn't be alive today."
I remember my heart racing, and feeling like I was in an echo chamber, as she continued.

"I felt the presence of God, and I knew I was leaving, and His peace was so compelling, I wanted to go. I heard you call me back, and I was torn, not knowing which way I should go."

Today, as I was writing these words, I called Rickie and asked her again,

"Tell me about your 'door of heaven' experience."

"The peace and love I experienced was incomparable, unequaled. I was bathed in His love and majesty. The glory of God, His peace and love, were so overwhelming I did not want to leave His presence. There are no words to describe how loved and cherished I felt. His peace penetrated my soul and nourished it. I get goose bumps thinking about it. It was wondrous!"

We discovered more to the story when Rickie returned home. I am so glad I was glued to my wristwatch that day with Rickie, making sure she took drinks every ten minutes, and recording in my brain the times of all my mental nursing notes. The rest of the story coincides precisely with my mental nursing notes.

Tasha, college student, was at home while we were hiking. On the evening of our second day on the Wonderland Trail, Tasha heard her mom calling from the front yard. She reasoned, "That is impossible. My mom is hiking in the mountains."

She heard the call again. It was so real that she actually opened up the front door and stepped out to check if her mom was in the yard. Once inside, she felt like something was seriously wrong. Falling on her knees, she knelt before God and prayed for her mom. Looking at the clock, it was 7:00 p.m, the exact time when Rickie had mumbled into the sleeping bag, "I am not afraid to die."

Since that close encounter with death, Rickie says, "I absolutely have no fear of death."

I say, "Praise God for answered prayer."

And then there was Sue...

Chapter 19

PROMISE

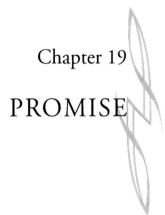

Oh Lord, we are lumps of clay on Your potter's wheel.

Mold us, fill us, use us; this we pray.

SUE FROM (HER last name rhymes with PROM) was an acquaintance from high school, whom I met again in my early years of raising children. She was a great model in living a life to the glory of God.

Her home was like a huge funnel, where gifts poured in and gifts poured out. Both of us struggled to provide clothes for our four children. I remember visiting her when she took me upstairs and pulled clothes out of her children's closets.

"Here, take this; and this too."

My arms heaped with clothes, I tried stopping her.

"Sue, this is plenty. Really. We are fine."

"No, you have to take this outfit, and here, this will be perfect for your kids."

Friends gave her bags of apples, which she turned into applesauce. After doing all the work of making the applesauce,

"Oh, and you need to take these jars of applesauce. They are really good."

"But, Sue, you can keep these. You need these for your own family."

"We have plenty."

Carrying bags of clothing and jars of applesauce, I returned home. When I brought something to give her, I returned home with more than I had given. She told one of her friends, "Whenever I feel really poor, I go in and find things to give away."

Sue and I were both pregnant with our youngest daughters at the same time. She delighted in all the pregnancy pains, because they meant she was going to have a baby. Two weeks after little Lisa was born, the "pregnancy pains" turned out to be something else. Doctors opened her up to discover her abdomen full of cancer, with cancer extending into her liver. The surgeon, who believed she would not live long enough to even be discharged from the hospital, told Sue she had, at most, six months to live. He could not tell a mother of a two-week-old baby that she had only a few days left of her life. Surgeons removed as much cancer as possible, gave her a hysterectomy, and sewed her up.

Nine and a half years and eleven surgeries later, Sue outlived her short life expectancy. During those years she thanked God for the remissions and clung to the hope that she would see all her children graduate from high school. Our high school graduating class raised money to buy her a white car and fly her and her children to Disneyland. Someone dumped a load of firewood in her backyard, and then stacked it in neat piles. And yet, people felt like they received more from Sue than they could ever give back to her, for Sue's deep love for Jesus spilled out in love to all who knew her.

Sue took delight in the little things of life. Who else cries tears of sadness when hanging up her last load of diapers on the clothesline outside? With her children toilet trained, she would no longer savor the sweetness of diapers blowing in the wind.

We gathered up our children for a weekend getaway in a beautiful home on Harstene Island. Having brought wood from home, she built her first beach fire. Remembering the huge fires my dad built on all our camping trips, this fire won the "cutest" award. She thrilled over the multitude of stars in the sky and magnificence of our Creator.

"Let's stand here until the tide comes in and puts out our fire. Wouldn't that be fun? I have never seen the tide put out a fire."

I looked at the sloping beach and mentally calculated we would be waiting for a couple hours. I was cold and the cute little fire we were huddled over was not generating noticeable heat. Not wanting to quench her enthusiasm, I mustered up,

"Great idea."

A while later, creativity came to our rescue.

"Let's help the tide, and move our fire closer to the water."

"Fabulous idea, Sue!"

A cute fire can be moved with ease. We slid it down to the water's edge and watched the tiny waves lap at our fire until it was totally out.

"Have you ever done this before?"

"No, Sue, it was a first."

Our trip to the beach was my last outing with Sue. Oscillating between remissions and new bouts with cancer, Sue's health declined. Visiting her in the hospital after one of her surgeries, we walked into her empty room. Staff could not immediately find her, for she was on another floor gazing at the babies through the nursery window. She loved babies and just looking at them through the glass windows energized her.

All smiles, she climbed back into the big hospital bed and laughed her way through a hospital lunch. The red Jell-O was her favorite. As conversation took a more serious twist, she jolted us when she stated,

"You know? If I were given a choice to live my life with cancer or without cancer, I think I would choose to live it with cancer. I have connected with so many people I never would have known, had I not been stricken with cancer."

During one of her surgical recoveries at home, when she was exceptionally weak, friends decided Sue needed a picnic. They spread out a red checkered tablecloth on the carpet and even sprinkled raisins around to represent ants. It was fun to surprise her with little things like indoor picnics, because Sue delighted in people, and appreciated the little things in life.

Her final hospital stay lasted for two and a half months before she went home to be with the Lord. Several friends rotated through shifts of staying in her hospital room so she would not be alone. On one visit, through her partly open door, I saw her kneeling on top of the bed, palms together with arms raised upward, as she poured out her prayers to God. On Halloween, she and Bryna and I told funny stories, invented games with candy treats, and laughed at everything.

Gradually the cancer devoured her. The day before she died, I slipped into her room and knelt before her bed. She was on her back, lying motionless, her body emaciated from the cancer. I felt her hand and there was no recognition that I was even in the room. And then I saw her lower lip move, as if she wanted to say something. I heard nothing. As I knelt beside her bed, I began praying through the twenty-third Psalm.

"The Lord is your shepherd, and you are His special Sue sheep. He loves you, Sue. And He is picking you up in His arms and holding you close to His chest."

I spoke slowly and quietly as I prayerfully moved through the psalm. In the pauses, I could see her lower lip move. She heard the words, and she was responding. Throughout my half-hour visit, as I knelt beside her, no other part of her body moved. There was no movement of fingers or feet; just her lower lip. Her desire of living until her son's November birthday had been fulfilled. Her time to be with Jesus was coming.

The next day her vital signs were irregular, and the family was called in. Sue lay motionless, her breathing stopping and starting. Too weak to even move a finger the previous day, she suddenly bolted upright in bed, looked straight ahead with a big smile and a radiant face filled with joy, and rejoiced, "Praise the Lord!"

Her focus was not on the people in the room, for she saw what no one else could see. Then she fell back onto her pillow. And then the instruments went dead. Sue passed from life into life.

I believe that Sue never saw death, but passed from life into life. She saw heaven before her heart rate monitor stopped. Jesus has taken away the sting of death.

When Bryna collapsed on the bathroom floor, did Jesus take away the sting of death for her? Did she experience unfathomable joy before her body went cold? Was she overcome with the love of Jesus? Was she watching from above when her dad was trying to resuscitate her?

One of Sue's favorite passages was 2 Timothy 4:7–8.

"I have fought the good fight,
I have finished the race,
I have kept the faith.
Now there is in store for me the crown of righteousness,
which the Lord, the righteous Judge,
will award to me on that day ..."

I want to love Jesus with all my heart, as she did, so that I can lavish love on others, as she so gloriously lavished. I want to fight the good fight, finish the race, and keep the faith. I want the last words out of my mouth to be: "Praise the Lord."

God has promised us a crown of righteousness.
We are His workmanship.
Heaven is for real.

SMALL GROUP QUESTIONS

CHAPTERS 1–3

Share a time when you saw God at work in your life.

Is God calling you to release a situation into his care?

When did God give you a "no" or "wait" response to your prayer?

Which verse in Psalm 139 speaks to you?

How would you answer, "Who is Jesus?"

Describe your artichoke of faith. What are your core beliefs?

CHAPTERS 4–6

In what says do we put God in a box?

Find scripture implying our importance to God

Share a surprise answer you received from prayer.

How has God been "God of the impossible" in your life?

Relate 1 John 1:9 to your own experiences.

How do we lose by failing to ask God?

CHAPTERS 7–9

Read II Corinthians 12:9. Share a time when you felt weak and God sustained you.

What prayers are inappropriate to take to our Holy, Almighty God of the universe? Why?

What are some questions on your list to God?

When have you suffered from feelings of inadequacy or abandonment by God?

How can we fulfill I Thessalonians 5:17 in our daily life?

What are the lies that keep us from praying?

CHAPTERS 10–12

Are you more prone to be independent and not ask for help, or to be overly needy? (Pray to God for a healthy balance).

Read John 3:16 – 18 and I John 1: 8-9. In what area of your life are you most tempted to dwell on self-condemnation?

What are some lies against you that you have had to combat? What truths can you claim to replace the lies?

What are some petty wars you need to relinquish or have relinquished?

When life beats you down, do you have the tendency to run to God or run away from Him? Why?

Read Jeremiah 17:9 and Proverbs 4:25. We have to guard our hearts, for our heart can be the well-spring of life or the well-spring of death. Share how you have had to fight against a root of bitterness.

CHAPTERS 13-15

How do you see Romans 8:28 at work in your life?

Who is in your hedge of protection? Does your hedge lead you into a deeper relationship with God?

Read Isaiah 61: 1-3. How has God brought into your life beauty for ashes, or gladness for mourning, or praise for despair?

Do you agree or disagree with the statement that people don't marry soul mates? Why?

Share a restoration story from your life.

What action steps are you taking or could you take in restoring a significant relationship?

CHAPTERS 16-19

What are some lessons from grief that you want to hang onto?

What are some things a person can do to keep from getting stuck in the grieving process?

What are possible lies that cause a person to flee from God's presence when life becomes painful?

How were you encouraged by Rickie's story?

How were you encouraged by Sue's story?

Explain your definition of "embracing God's grace."

BOOK CLUB QUESTIONS

How did the book speak to you?

What lessons in grieving over losses helped you?

Relate shepherd and sheep to the message of the book?

How would you define God's grace as portrayed in the book?

END NOTES:

Page 6 quotes from GOD'S SMUGGLER, by Brother Andrew with John and Elizabeth Sherrill. Published by Chosen Books, a division of Baker Book House Co. in Grand Rapids, Michigan 49516. Published 1967 and 2001. Quotes from pages 107, 108, 165, 166.

Page 32 reference to C.S. Lewis book MERE CHRISTIANITY, pages 55-56, published by Macmillan Publishing Co, Inc New York. Copyright 1943, 1945, 1952.

Page 67 reference to story from ANGELS by Billy Graham. Published by Word Publishing in Dallas, London, Vancouver, Melbourne. Copyright 1975, 1986 and 1994. Story from page 5 of the book.

Page 134–135 Permission granted to reprint *I Will Rise* written by Chris Tomlin.

SHARE YOUR COMMENTS

Marlys Johnson would appreciate receiving your comments, which you may submit by sending them to embracinggrace2013@gmail.com.

CPSIA information can be obtained at www.ICGtesting.com
Printed in the USA
LVOW08s2155220514

387023LV00004B/275/P